Do Nothing

無為

Do Nothing

INNER PEACE FOR EVERYDAY LIVING

Reflections on Chuang Tzu's Philosophy

Siroj Sorajjakool

TEMPLETON FOUNDATION PRESS
WEST CONSHOHOCKEN, PENNSYLVANIA

Templeton Foundation Press
300 Conshohocken State Road, Suite 550
West Conshohocken, PA 19428
www.templetonpress.org

Templeton Foundation Press helps intellectual leaders and others learn about science research on aspects of realities, invisible and intangible. Spiritual realities include unlimited love, accelerating creativity, worship, and the benefits of purpose in persons and in the cosmos.

Typeset and designed by Gopa and Ted2, Inc.

Library of Congress Cataloging-in-Publication Data

Sorajjakool, Siroj.
Do nothing : inner peace for everyday living : reflections on Chuang Tzu's philosophy / Siroj Sorajjakool.
p. cm.
Includes bibliographical references.
ISBN-13: 978-1-59947-153-2 (alk. paper)
ISBN-10: 1-59947-153-1 (alk. paper)
1. Zhuangzi. Nanhua jing. 2. Philosophy, Chinese.
I. Title. II. Title: Inner peace for everyday living.
BL1900.C576S87 2009
299.5'1482—dc22
2008031445

Printed in the United States of America

09 10 11 12 13 14   10 9 8 7 6 5 4 3 2 1

To my son, Chanchai Sorajjakool,
whose birth and life made me
reflect deeply on
the meaning of life
To my wife, Huiling Lee,
who lives the life of simplicity

and

To millions of ordinary people
who, in their ordinary ways,
make everyday living
possible

Contents

無為

Foreword

無為

WHAT HAPPENS when a committed Christian reads the classical writing of Taoism? Usually, not much. But when the Christian is already struggling with the question of meaning at a deep level and is truly open to wisdom in strange contexts and forms, a great deal. Because of Professor Sorajjakool's serious and deeply personal wrestling with the text, a great deal of Taoist wisdom comes to expression in this book in ways that, for the reader, is powerful and clear.

Those of us in the Abrahamic traditions are almost always moralists. We want to know what we *ought* to do. And we are very likely to have strong opinions about whether others are doing what they *should*. When we Christians are told that we *should* avoid legalism we usually define legalism as a misuse of law. We add this "should" to the other "shoulds" that make up our moral arsenal.

Although we have had many teachers who have explained to us that Paul's opposition to legalistic thinking and living went much deeper than this, we have trouble believing that he really wanted to abolish the role of dos and don'ts in our lives. We assume that he could not have meant *that*. So we continue to find alternative explanations. We assume he must have meant that law should be tempered with mercy. Or he must have meant that we are free from the dietary and ceremonial laws of the Jews, but certainly not from the Ten Commandments. The fact that Paul used one of the Ten Commandments to explain the deadliness of the legalistic life does not deter us from interpreting Paul to fit our preconceived notions.

Why talk about Paul in a book about Taoism? Paul was certainly not a Taoist. Yet at a deep level, the Chinese sages and Paul were responding to the same kind of problem, the deep hold on conscientious people of a need to distinguish good from bad, right from wrong. The facts that Paul's writings have been canonized and that Paul is recognized as the greatest Christian thinker have not sufficed to persuade Christians to take him seriously. Perhaps if we encounter something similar in a very different tradition we can be shaken from our commitment to legalistic thinking. Perhaps if we can see in a very different tradition that the rejection of legalism is not the promotion of destructive actions, we can see this also in our own.

Some Christians suppose that the positive function of encountering other forms of wisdom is to understand and appreciate more deeply the wisdom of our own. Thus far I have written as if that were what a Christian might gain from this book. We *can* gain that, and that is a great deal. But Professor Sorajjakool does not obscure what is truly distinctive in his Taoist sources, what is truly different from our Christian tradition including Paul. For Paul, as for Jesus, the alternative to obedience to law is the life of love. For Taoism, the alternative is a kind of absence or nothingness or emptiness. If one seeks for equivalent ideas in the Christian tradition, one must turn to some of the mystics, but even there what one finds is not quite the same.

The reader of this book will be drawn into a deep understanding of this different alternative. The Christian reader will not be told just how, if at all, to integrate the wisdom offered by Taoist sages into Christian life and thought. Probably it is best to begin with life, practicing a Taoist response in situations where one finds it truly beneficial. Even if the texts do not speak of love, the Christian may find that Taoist methods help those they love as well as themselves. Even if the texts do not speak of bringing into being a better social order, one may find that acting in the way they invite has some such results.

Such experiences will not end the questions about how to relate the two traditions. But they may assure us that their relation is more one of complementarity than of contradiction. They may assure faithful Christians that their faithfulness does not close them to wisdom, wherever that may be found.

John B. Cobb Jr.

Acknowledgments

無為

LIFE MOVES according to the flow of its natural gravity. People come and go, events take place, thoughts and ideas intersect and intertwine, forming new concepts and modifying previous understanding. Life does not run in a linear rational process, and for this very reason, what is written in this book comes about through this process. My depression, my anxiety, my shadow, my achievements, my rewards, my parents, my siblings, my wife, my son, and my cats, these are integral parts of this journey. Without them, the process will never be what it is. There are people who have been intentional in this particular reflection on nothingness, and I wish to thank each of them. My colleague, Professor James Walters, offered very helpful suggestions on the chapter dealing with ethics of Chuang Tzu. Professor Roger Ames of the University of Hawai'i was kind enough to spend time reflecting on Chuang Tzu's and Eastern approaches to the understanding of reality. Professor Fabrizio Pregadio of Stanford University invited me out for lunch. We engaged in a wonderful conversation on Chuang Tzu, ethics, and the text. Dr. Richard Young offered numerous insights into the psychology of nothingness that not only influenced my thinking process but also my life in a meaningful way. Dr. Wesley Amundson was among the first to introduce me to the art of doing nothing and its spiritual meaning. To my colleague, Professor Carla Gober, for her profound wisdom on the ordinariness of life and for numerous conversations on life's meaning. To my wife, Huiling Lee, who taught me the importance of simplicity. To Dr. Gerald Winslow, who is always supportive and encouraging. To Bryn Seyle, whose perspective in life has enhanced my spiritual journey in the spirit of Chuang Tzu. I wish to thank Karen Clausen for her assistance in copyediting the original manuscript. Thanks also to Ulrike R. Guthrie for her very insightful editorial suggestions and recommendations. And thanks to my cat, Sigmund, whose pathological temperament brought so much joy to my life.

Do Nothing

無為

Introduction

無為

The whole world's praise could not bring pride to Sung Jung-tzu; neither could their condemnation, disappointment. There is no self for the Perfect; no merit for the Holy; no fame for the Sage.

—CHUANG TZU

WHAT IF MOST of what we have been told about life and most of what makes us work so hard isn't true? What if it isn't true that people who do well in school are smart, that smart people become successful, that successful people are happy, that happy people are respected by society, and that to step beyond the societal boundary is to be an aberration? We live our lives believing these statements are the formula for a satisfying and gratifying existence, but what if they aren't true? What if life has a life of its own and its path is nonlinear? Intelligence does not always mean success. Happiness cannot be determined mechanically. Society is not qualified to define aberration. And the mystical power of heaven remains very much a part of life. Where do we go from here?

I have spent most of my life trying to avoid failure. Success, I was taught, is the key. When I was eight, my third-grade teacher and her friends read an exam paper I had written and laughed with great amusement. I did not know why it was so amusing, but apparently it was. Even now, I do not want to know what I actually wrote. Whatever it was, at the time I did not want to be embarrassed again and again, so I invested my energy in public compliance. Yet after numerous attempts at inventing and reinventing myself for public consumption, I still find myself at the margin. Where does it end?

I have heard people say, "I go to work, and I am not successful enough. I go to school, and I am not smart enough. I play, and I am not fast enough. Then I come home and wonder why my kids are not like my neighbor's kids who top their classes, play violin, sing in the choirs, join honor programs, invest in stock markets, and compete at national sports stadiums."

It seems as if there is always something more that we ought to do. Where we are in life is never enough. We keep hearing voices saying, "You are not good enough. Be more productive, more successful, more cheerful, more charming." The word "more" is exhausting and yet very tempting. It judges, evaluates, and assesses. It is seductive, persuasive, and convincing.

From a young age I learned that life was always about getting "there," that something more always existed "there," and that if you really wanted to find what you wanted in life, you had to be "there." No matter what you did, you should not stay "here." You were not to remain "here" or wait "here." You had to go on, move on, keep fighting until you got "there" because "here" was not good enough.

It's funny how this "not good enough" message becomes a fertile soil for commercialism. Sellers tell you that you are too fat, and they sell you books, DVDs, and diet programs so that you can be thin. They tell you that you are stupid, and they sell you products to make you feel smarter. They tell you that you are too poor, and they sell you methods to make you richer. Therapists tell you that you have an inferiority complex and that you need to pay them so they can tell you that you're okay.

We are haunted by a sense that what we have and who we are are insufficient. This sense intensifies our hope that when we get "there," everything will be all right. But when we do get "there," it doesn't feel like we've gotten anywhere. The journey continues because "there" will always be there. It is never here where we currently are. It is not "now" but "then" and "there." Always "there." As life moves from one category to another, multiplying standards and norms, the experience of pain intensifies. "There" is always there.

Yet somewhere, in the midst of this busyness of our striving, the spiritual self begs us to pause, to rest, and to step back. Somewhere deep inside us, a voice invites us to ponder the transforming power of silence. The spiritual dimension, the divine play that transcends our human categorical understanding of life, moves in the opposite direction. In the urge for more, it asks for less. In the strife for height, it asks for depth. In the search for something, it asks for nothing. Here resides the salvation promised by the wisdom of religious traditions from generation to generation.

The best of life is not a fight for more but a movement toward nothing, toward silence. It is not a struggle to get "there" but the courage to remain "here." J. Krishnamurti writes, "In the light of silence, all problems are dissolved."[1] Speaking of life's struggle, he argues:

> Does it not come about when there is this constant urge to be something, that desire for a result, the desire for self-improvement, the desire to achieve a certain noble action? As long as one is competitive, ambitious, there must be disturbance, there must be conflict. Without beginning near, we want to go far, but we can go far only when we begin very near. And beginning near is freedom from ambition, from wanting to be something, from the desire to be successful, to be recognized, to be famous.[2]

I remember the evening that I watched Mel Gibson's *Hamlet*. At the end of the movie, I had learned one line: "To be or not to be. That is the question," and it became my obsession. I pondered, cogitated, and meditated over it. "What does it mean to be?" I wondered. Stumbling upon *Being and Nothingness* by Jean-Paul Sartre, I had a dim ray of hope that perhaps his profound reflections could offer insights. "Now I will surely discover the meaning of being," I thought to myself. However, after the first twenty pages I had learned nothing, and put the book back on the shelf. I continued to search for other ways "to be."

As an idealistic youth, I thought "to be" meant to reach for the stars, to think big, to be successful, to achieve, to climb the highest mountain, and (metaphorically) to swim across the deepest ocean. I was inspired by the song, "The Impossible Dream" that calls us to bear unbearable sorrow and to run where brave people dare not go. I now realize that I do not want to run where the brave dare not go. Actually I do not even run in the first place! I hate running! So where do I go from here in my quest for being?

While I was under stress, working hard toward my doctorate, my brother, being the kind brother that he is, bought me a joke book to add flavor to my life. I came across this story that has since become my favorite:

> Bailey had left his job as a successful marketing man, determined to find the meaning of life. After six months of reading and meditation, he learned of a lama who had spent the last thirty years alone on the top of a mountain in Tibet. Everything he heard about this holy man convinced Bailey that only by visiting the mountaintop could he learn the true meaning of life.
>
> He sold everything he had, flew to Tibet, and hired a team of guides to lead him to the mountain. They took him halfway up, then explained that he would have to make the rest of the trek by himself.
>
> Obsessed with his goal, Bailey continued on, climbing for hours each day and eating only enough to keep up his strength. After ten days of solitary climbing, he reached the top of the mountain. There, sitting cross-legged and facing the sun, was the lama he had come to see.

> He carefully made his way to the holy man's spot, stood in front of him, and made a little bow with his head. The lama looked up at his visitor.
>
> "Sir," Bailey said, "I have sacrificed everything, even risked my life, to reach you. I know you are the only one who can tell me the secret of life."
>
> The lama stared at Bailey for several minutes. Finally, he spoke. "Life," he said hoarsely, "is a stream."
>
> Bailey waited, but the man said nothing more. In desperation, Bailey broke the silence. "What do you mean, 'life is a stream'?" The old man raised his eyebrows and shrugged his shoulders. "All right, all right," he said, "life is not a stream."[3]

The humor is profound. The lama's second statement makes a stream real. "All right, life is not a stream." Life may be a stream. Life may not be a stream. One has to decide. There is no basis except that existential leap into the future. There is nothing, and when one enters this nothingness, one realizes that emptiness makes the flow possible. Nothingness makes life flexible. As Lao Tzu once said:

> We hammer wood for a house,
> but it is the inner space
> that makes it livable[4]

Chuang Tzu tells a story of a bird named P'eng. His back is as large as Mount T'ai, and his wings are like clouds filling up the sky. "He beats the whirlwind, leaps into the air, and rises up ninety thousand *li*, cutting through the clouds and mist, shouldering the blue sky, and then he turns his eyes south and prepares to journey to the southern darkness."[5]

Small people laugh at the story, asking, "How is that possible?" But the sage knows better. The sage knows that one can rise up ninety thousand *li* and journey to the southern darkness. Sung Jung-tzu is one such person. "The whole world's praise could not bring pride to Sung Jung-tzu; neither could their condemnation, disappointment." One can rise ninety thousand *li* and dig the darkest deep when the profoundness of nothing fills the soul. Without the empty space, one cannot fly.

This book tells of a personal journey into the profundity of nothingness and the art of doing nothing. It is about a journey in life that finally comes to the realization that in the end, spirituality is the essence of our souls, and that the most important thing in life may be to remain in the presence of God. It is about "getting there without going anywhere." It is about movement in stillness, going by staying, knowing through unlearning. It is about staying that fills the sky and the ocean. On a number of occasions, I have told my students that my life's aim is to do nothing. And this doing nothing may be the most important aspect of my spiritual journey. Here is the beginning of my journey, the start of the ninety thousand *li*.

This book is not intended as an exegesis of Chuang Tzu but a journey consisting of conversations between my personal narratives and the text. I write as a Christian who has been deeply influenced by Chuang Tzu. His wisdom and perspectives in life have given me new insights into the meaning and understanding of spirituality. My aim is to explore Chuang Tzu's understanding of nothing and to let this nothing be the beginning of the journey. More specifically, I will reflect on Chuang Tzu's nothingness and his critique of our tendency toward discrimination and categorization in an attempt to help us understand how we come to define who we are, and hence the meaning of being. It is from within this context that the term spirituality is used. In this book I limit my usage of the term spirituality to one dimension, the quest for the meaning of self within the broader reality of life.

The first chapter of this book looks at the life of Chuang Tzu in its historical context and examines his approach to life. Chapter two introduces Chuang Tzu and Lao Tzu's approach to the Way and their belief that it is not understanding that will guide our path. The world tells us to seek, accumulate, acquire, and obtain in our path toward the ultimate, but Chuang Tzu believes that when you think you know the way, you should not follow it. One prerequisite to his approach is to deconstruct the way we are used to being, to move beyond the "this" and the "that." Chapter three is an exploration of the term "nothing" through Chuang Tzu's use of the useless. "Nothing" does not end in just nothing. "Nothing" makes it possible for us to leap ninety thousand *li*. This understanding of the causal relation between leaping and nothing I discuss in chapter four. Chapters five to chapter seven contain my personal exploration of nothingness as it relates to everyday living. They discuss the art of doing nothing, the nothing of love, and some more practical and ethical implications of nothing.

The book concludes with the image of a person who practices nondoing.

This is my journey into nothing. It is the path through remaining and not struggling to get somewhere. The unknown path of Chuang Tzu is paradoxical. Hence it is the journey and not clarity, the conversation and not the discussion that are being expressed in the following pages. Any logical clarity will only be a betrayal to Chuang Tzu's literary approach, which was constructed to speak to the psyche and the soul.

1. Chuang Tzu

無為

There was a man with a chopped foot in Lu, Wang T'ai,
who had as many disciples in his retinue as Confucius himself.
Ch'ang Chi asked Confucius, "Wang T'ai had his foot chopped off,
but the disciples in his train divide Lu down the middle with yours.
When he stands up he doesn't teach, when he sits down he doesn't
talk things over, yet they go to him empty and come away full.
Is there indeed a wordless teaching, or a heart which is whole
though the body is deformed? What man is this?"

—CHUANG TZU

Chuang Tzu has the habit of introducing people with physical "defects" to the text, and Wang T'ai is one of these characters. Wang T'ai has a chopped foot, and in Wang T'ai's character, Chuang Tzu shows the contrast between what society calls defective and normative. Even though Wang T'ai is defective, he has many followers. What can be so fascinating about a man with a chopped foot? There must be something "defectively" fascinating about Wang T'ai that draws people. His wordless teaching fills hearts and his deformity makes people whole. Characters such as Wang T'ai are Chuang Tzu's tools for bringing readers to the dimension of depth in their lives. Their wordless teaching can help people realize wholeness in a deformed body. Perhaps even in pathology there can be completeness if we are able to hear what is not said and be taught by wordless teachings. Perhaps we can recognize and find such wholeness if we can remain within this ambiguity and allow such a recognition to emerge through paradoxes.

It is precisely through paradoxes and ambiguity that Chuang Tzu helps us experience such wholeness. For example, concluding "In the World of Men," in the Inner Chapters he writes, "All men know the use of the useful, but nobody knows the use of the useless."[1] Can the useless become useful? What has uselessness got to do with usefulness? Chuang Tzu forces us to rethink our normative definitions. Can there be any use in uselessness? Perhaps, if we understood how the perceptual world is being created and how this creation binds us to its world. Likewise, Chuang Tzu says, "A road is made by people walking on it; things are so because they are called so. What makes them so? Making them so makes them so. What makes them not so? Making them not so makes them not so."[2] But is "so" really "so" because we make it so? This is the very question that Chuang Tzu raises for us.

Chuang Tzu was not the only person who raised this type of question. Before Chuang Tzu was the Old Boy, Lao Tzu.

Lao Tzu

Many stories surround the life of Lao Tzu,[3] or Old Tan (Old Boy), especially regarding his authorship of the *Tao Te Ching*. According to the *Records of the Historian*, he was a native of Ch'u (which is now Honan Province), his family name was Li, and he served as a custodian for the imperial archives. According to legend, he was born with white hair. At an old age he retired to the West, and at the request of the gatekeeper, Lao Tzu wrote more than five thousand words on the Way (*Tao*) and its Virtue (*Te*).[4]

According to one account, Confucius sought Lao Tzu's wisdom by paying him a visit. During the interview,

> Li (Lao-tzu) said to K'ung (Confucius): The men about whom you talk are dead, and their bones are mouldered to dust; only their words are left. Moreover, when the superior man gets his opportunity, he mounts aloft; but when the time is against him, he is carried along by the force of circumstances. I have heard that a good merchant, though he have rich treasures safely stored, appears as if he were poor; and that the superior man, though his virtue be complete, is yet to outward seeming stupid. Put away your proud air and many desires, your insinuating habit and wild will. They are of no advantage to you;—this is all I have to tell you.

After the interview, Confucius was known to have said:

> I know how birds can fly, fishes swim, and animals run. But the runner may be snared, the swimmer hooked, and the flyer shot by the arrow. But there is the dragon:—I cannot tell how he mounts on the wind through the clouds, and rises to heaven. Today I have seen Lao-tzu, and can only compare him to the dragon.[5]

During Lao Tzu's time, the country was in chaos politically, sociologically, and religiously. People were searching for a way out of chaos. They wanted order and structure, and they were searching for the Way. They were looking for the Tao. In Chinese characters, the Tao is represented by a path and a person walking in it. People were yearning for a person who could point them to the Tao. In the midst of this quest the gatekeeper of the emperor's archives noticed an old wise man. It was during this period that Lao Tzu wrote his five thousand words on the Way of virtue (The Tao Te Ching). Some like to call it the Natural Way or the Way of Nature because Nature, to Lao Tzu, is One, eternal, spontaneous, and nameless. Lao Tzu taught that to live in accordance with the Way means embracing simplicity, spontaneity, tranquility, weakness, and nonaction (*wu wei*).[6] Others, like Herrlee Creel, call Lao Tzu's Taoism "purposive" as an attempt to distinguish it from that of Chuang Tzu's, which is, to Creel, "contemplative." It is purposive in that it "is concerned with how one should respond to the world" or, in Arthur Waley's words, it "is a description of how the Sage through the practice of Tao acquires the power of ruling without being known to rule."[7] To many, Lao Tzu's Taoism teaches leaders how to lead effectively and how to live together in a community. I like to think that for Lao Tzu, Tao is a way of being, a path to true spirituality.

There is yet another sage: Chuang Tzu.

Chuang Tzu

Not much is known about Chuang Tzu except from historian Ssu-ma Ch'ien's (145?–89? BCE) account of him in the *Records of the Historian*. According to him, Chuang Tzu's personal name was Chou (Chuang Chou) or Master Chou, he once served as "an official in the lacquer garden" in a place called Meng, and he once declined an invitation to serve as a prime minister. Ssu-ma Ch'ien dated Chuang Tzu to the reigns of King Hui of Liang or Wei (370–319 BCE) and King Hsuan of Ch'i (319–301 BCE).[8]

Chaung Tzu's Taoism is transcendental in nature. It is spontaneous, intuitive, private, and unconventional. In describing the differences between Lao Tzu and Chaung Tzu, Wing-Tsit Chan writes:

> The Tao in Lao Tzu is still worldly, whereas in Chaung Tzu it becomes transcendental. While Lao Tzu emphasizes the difference between glory and disgrace, strength and weakness, and so forth, and advocates the tender values, Chuang Tzu identifies them all. Lao Tzu aims at reform, but Chuang Tzu prefers to "travel beyond the mundane world."[9]

His emphasis on transcendence brought with it criticism from various schools of thought. Confucians said that he was "prejudiced in favor of Nature and does not know man." Ssu-ma Ch'ien described his work as "empty talk not based on facts . . . primarily aimed at pleasing himself and useless to rulers of men." Chu Hsi, a leading neo-Confucian, complained, "Lao Tzu still wanted to do something, but Chuang Tzu did not want to do anything at all. He even said that he knew what to do but just did not want to do it."[10]

Chuang Tzu's Methods

Chu Hsi's critique of Chuang Tzu's "doing nothing" may appear reasonable, but deeper reflection reminds us that his approach has significant theological and spiritual implications. For example: think of the problem of pain. To a large extent, it is a conceptual construction and one that people have typically attempted to deal with by creating new ways (of being) and redefining definitions. So for Confucius the way out of chaos was filial piety, whereas Mo Ti's way was the way of love, and Shang Yang preferred the way of disciplines. All these problem-solving methods seek a person's social, moral, and ethical reformation. But Chuang Tzu thought otherwise. In describing Chuang Tzu's realization, translator Burton Watson writes:

> He believes that they were ills only because man recognized them as such. If man would once forsake his habit of labeling things good or bad, desirable or undesirable, then the man-made ills, which are the product of man's purposeful

> and value-ridden actions, would disappear and the natural ills that remain would no longer be seen as ills, but as an inevitable part of the course of life. Thus, in Chuang Tzu's eyes, man is the author of his own suffering and bondage, and all his fears spring from the web of values created by himself alone.[11]

How does one help others see that pain is their own creation? Why would anyone create pain for himself or herself? It does not seem to make sense. And yet this is precisely the problem: we turn that which is nonsensical into something sensible. Hence making sense of the nonsensical is Chuang Tzu's task, a difficult task indeed. According to Watson, Chuang Tzu attempts to make sense of nonsense through three methods. First, he uses paradoxes or nonsensical remarks to help others come to their senses: "Where can I find a man who has forgotten words so I can have a word with him?"[12] Second, he starts his conversation through rationality and leads the readers to total pointlessness. Third, Chuang Tzu uses humor so one can laugh in the face of the unknown and maintain sanity. Indeed, as Robert Allinson comments, "Chuang Tzu is attempting to force the reader to disengage the conceptual or analytic powers of his or her mind . . . and at the same time to engage the intuitive or aesthetic functions of the mind."[13] Yet, Allinson continues, to read Chuang Tzu's work does not result in a cognitive analytical conceptualization, but rather an inner transformation of the self because when the aesthetic is evoked,

> It grasps something but it is not able to state what it grasps in words. That the question is poetically framed in its comparison of language with the chirping of birds, arouses the aesthetic function, which is charmed and attracted by the poetic imagery. One side of the mind is made to feel helpless. The other side of the mind is aroused to action.[14]

Chuang Tzu's paradoxes and ambiguity are designed to speak directly to the suffering soul. Perhaps we can say that his is a psychodynamic approach to philosophy.

How then can one cease being the author of one's own suffering? Chuang Tzu suggests it is by doing nothing. This concept will be explored in other chapters. But before we move further, a word about the text itself.

The Text

The present version of Chuang Tzu's text is believed to have been compiled by Liu An in 122 BCE during the Han Dynasty and later edited by neo-Taoist Kuo Hsiang in approximately 300 CE. Kuo Hsiang divided the text into thirty-three sections and grouped these thirty-three sections into three categories. The first seven chapters are called the "inner chapters." The next fifteen sections he called the "outer chapters." And the last portion he called "miscellaneous chapters." Most scholars seem to think that the first seven chapters were written by Chuang Tzu himself, and for this reason these inner chapters are most widely translated. The outer chapters and miscellaneous chapters are believed to have been written by commentators seeking to expand on Chuang Tzu's work.

Why Chuang Tzu?

In his introduction to his translation of Chuang Tzu's writings, Victor Mair mourned the fact that very few Americans, except within the scholarly circles, have heard of *The Chuang Tzu* and "much less experienced the thrill of dipping inside its covers."[15] And while Lao Tzu's *Tao Te Ching* gains popularity within the American culture, Mair sees it as a Taoist fast-food. "*The Chuang Tzu,* on the other hand, is more like a banquet or a buffet—you are obliged to spend more time savoring its tremendous variety of delightful dishes, and of course you have to pay a bit more because it is bigger."[16]

Commenting on the depth of Chuang Tzu's paradoxes, Victor Mair states:

> The sublime wisdom of *The Chuang Tzu* is imparted to us by poking holes in our conventional knowledge and assumptions about what is good and bad. It accomplishes all of this, furthermore with a divine sense of humor throughout. *The Chuang Tzu* deals with very heavy stuff, but it does so with a feather-light touch.[17]

Perhaps through this featherlight touch, the burden of life that weights heavily on us will not remain ever the same. Chuang Tzu invites us to an alternate reality. And through his wordless teaching helps us realize a world that sits in our souls waiting to be discovered. “Words,” writes Chuang Tzu, “are for catching ideas; once you’ve caught the idea, you can forget about the words. When can I find a person who knows how to forget about words so that I can have a few words with him?”[18] So let’s have a few words with Chuang Tzu.

2. The Way

無為

The Way gave him a face; Heaven gave him a form.
He doesn't let likes or dislikes get in and do him harm.
You, now—you treat your spirit like an outside.
You wear out your energy, leaning on a tree and moaning,
slumping at your desk and dozing—
Heaven picked out a body for you and you use it
to gibber about "hard" and "white."

—CHUANG TZU

PEOPLE SEEK THE WAY in an attempt to find relief from suffering. Yet Lao Tzu tells us in the very first chapter of *Tao Te Ching* that we do not really know the Way. If we knew it, it would not be the right Way. This is a strange answer to a very valid question. If we do not know the Way, how can we walk in the right path? If we do not know the Way, how can we find relief? And yet not knowing is what both Lao Tzu and Chuang Tzu insist upon. The Way is that of undifferentiated Reality.[1] Lao Tzu describes this Way as a name for whatever happens. "The *Tao* principle is what happens of itself [*tzu-jan*]."[2] Or in Chuang Tzu's words, "The Way gave him a face; Heaven gave him a form."[3] The problem is that we like to gibber about "hard" and "white." Why are we so obsessed with this dichotomy, with trying to arrive at rational, logical conclusions about life?

Logic and Alienation

We grow up with the notion that the real is rational, logical, and reasonable. The Way, therefore, is to be known. Then, once we know, we can rest assured that everything would turn out all right; the world would be a better place. There would be peace, progress, and prosperity. The problem is, we have not thought hard enough. The problem really is, however, that there is a flaw in our logical analysis. The problem has to do with the unreasonableness of the nonrational people. We have to think harder. We have to help others become more sensible. The Way is to be known. The unknown is the root of evil. So we set before us the task of making rational sense of reality and of God. So we search for a rational God. So we search through our rationality to find this God. We seek rational constructions of theological systems. And we keep pursuing, not realizing that we are limited and finite, that reality and God are much bigger than that which we can conceive and realize, not realizing that there are dimensions within us that lie beyond the realm of logic and reasoning. Hence although rationality plays an important role in contributing to the development of our civilization, it also has a shortcoming. In *The Dwelling Place of Wisdom*, Raimundo Panikkar warns:

> It is almost perverse how we are bombarded by information as if we needed the latter for living life as humans. Whatever we call scientific progress is nothing other than the expansion of specialized sciences that divide themselves more and more in order to enlighten us less and less. The real problem, however, is that this method has become a serious requirement for us and we now regard its analytical path as "natural." . . . We find ever more subdivisions, more discoveries, and come to more interesting and attractive results. In the end, however, we are unable to put things together—like a child who has taken apart a toy. We are no longer able to play because we are too occupied by the analysis of the various parts into which we have dissected reality. . . . The holistic attitude has been lost because the person has been reduced to reason, reason to intellect, and intellect to the ability to classify and to formulate laws about how things work.[4]

As a consequence of our logical analysis and rational thinking under Descartes' dictum "*Cogito, ergo sum,*" the world was divided into subject and object.[5] The "I" was the subject and the world was the object. Through logical reasoning, the I could penetrate the structure of the object and control nature. The I was not a part of nature. It had been set apart to conquer the world. This could be achieved through logical reasoning. But Nature refused to be conquered by reason, and analysis may lead to alienation.

Nature refused to be the object of human's analysis but claimed human as part of the whole organism.

The alienation we are experiencing is perhaps a warning sign informing our hearts that Nature transcends logic; that Nature cannot be captured by logic; that any attempt to capture Nature by logic ends in uprooting self from its very nature. This warning sign leads us to greater curiosity of the nature of Nature. Why can't we capture Nature with logic and analysis?[6]

Paradoxes

A man went fishing, and a bystander observed him measuring every fish he caught. If it was longer than eight inches, he would throw it away. When asked what he was doing, the fisherman replied, "My frying pan is only eight inches wide." To limit reality to its usefulness is to miss the whole picture. Rationality forms part of reality, but reality cannot be reduced to rationality. There is more to reality than logic. Perhaps reality is not to be scrutinized but observed. Through observation, the Chinese discovered that there is polarity in Nature. Nature is not either/or but both/and. There is no black without white, and no light without darkness. There is no goodness without badness, and no right without wrong. There is no East without West, nor depth without height. There is no strength without weakness, nor sadness without joy. There is no *yin* without *yang*. Nature embraces both, maintaining the two opposites and keeping them in tension. Hence any effort to logically analyze Nature only uproots the self from Nature. So Western technology seeks to make the world a better place, but as

Alan Watts points out, it is fruitless to seek pleasure without pain, wealth without poverty, and health without sickness. By interfering with a complex system of relationships we do not understand, we create more problems than we resolve—and this is because we do not understand that Nature contains opposites.[7] C. S. Song in *Theology from the Womb of Asia* quotes a poem that reflects this oppositional Asian understanding of Nature:

> Two moons I see,
> The same in shape, yet different in feature.
>
> The one's just in the sky
> Decked in a gown of bird-plumes.
> She does not stint her favours,
> Her gold and silver spread o'er all the earth.
> She does not forget the tiles on the palace-roof.
> And the Three Lakes brim and glisten with her
> beauty.
> Over the clouds she leaps, over the tree-tops,
> And hides herself in green shades of the vine.
> Even the fish within the lakes are rapt!
> And yet she has a flaw . . .
> The naughty habit of becoming thin:
> Sometimes the sparks of stars are seen aloft
> But not her round enchanting countenance.
> And though she may return at other seasons
> This absence is a torture too excessive.
>
> Another moon there is you cannot see,
> Despite the splendour of her radiance.

She also has her dimple smiles
And grace of movement;
She's no less generous than the other moon. . . .
What a pity that you cannot see my garden!
Sublime her sorcery,
Kindling and quickening my ecstasies:
I love her sudden swell of silver waves
Leaping with melodies of silver bells,
Even her foam, blown white like horses' tails,
Fostered more tenderly than deep-sea pearls.
A full and perfect moon
Who never wanes.
Whenever I close these eyes of mine
She rises and sails into the heavens.[8]

There is the external moon with all its beauty, and yet it has its flaw. It gets into the naughty habit of becoming thin. Yet there is another moon deep within us. It is the moon that recognizes eternity in temporality; as C. S. Song states, "We are believers in life with its sorrows and joys, despairs and hopes. The cosmic moon and the moon in our hearts become united to rekindle our faith in eternity amid a world of temporality."[9] This tension of the two opposites as part of nature is also present in our psyche. According to Carl Jung, our psyche is constantly pointing us to the essential core of our humanity, which contains both good and evil, light and shadow, anima and animus, strength and weakness, the conscious and the unconscious.[10] Our psyche is begging us to embrace the good and the bad, the light and the shadow, the strength and weakness within each of us.[11]

Lao Tzu explains:

> When everyone knows beauty as beautiful,
> there is already ugliness;
> When everyone knows good as goodness,
> there is already evil.
> "To be" and "not to be" arise mutually;
> Difficult and easy are mutually realized;
> Long and short are mutually contrasted;
> High and low are mutually posited; . . .
> Before and after are in mutual sequence.[12]

The Way

It would be a mistake to think that by understanding the polarity of nature we have come to know the Way. In Fung Yu-lan's translation of the opening passage of *Tao Te Ching* we find the phrase, "The *Tao* that can be *Tao*-ed is not the invariable *Tao*." Or we can say, "The Way that can be wayed is not the eternal Way."[13] This paradoxical nature of Tao is puzzling. How can we learn that which we cannot name? How can we walk the way that is uncharted? How can we know that which cannot be known?

The Way is one and the One includes all. It cannot be defined in words. Neither is it a concept. To this, Chuang Tzu writes, "It may be attained but not seen."[14] Commenting on this notion, Alan Watts writes: "Simply because we know intuitively that there is a dimension of ourselves and of nature which eludes us because it is too close, too general, and too all-embracing to be singled out as a particular object."[15] The Tao is "too close" because it is a part of us and therefore it escapes our knowing. The Tao and its pattern escape us because they are ourselves, and we are, too. In the words of Zenrin Kushu: "Like a sword that cuts but cannot cut itself; like an eye that sees but cannot see itself."[16] Tao is not a place for us to get to. It is not a concept to grasp. It is not a state to be attained. In chapter 47 of *Tao Te Ching,* Lao Tzu writes:

> The world may be known
> Without leaving the house;
> The Way may be seen
> Apart from the windows.
> The further you go,
> The less you will know.
>
> Accordingly, the Wise Man
> Knows without going,
> Sees without seeing,
> Does without doing.[17]

So what is this Tao that we cannot know? The Tao just is. Nature is. In being what it is, Nature penetrates everything:

> O the great Way o'er flows and spreads on every side!
> All being comes from it; No creature is denied.
> But having called them forth, it calls not one its own.
> It feeds and clothes them all and will not be their lord.[18]

In penetrating everything, it embraces everything:

> The Way is a void, used but never filled:
> An abyss it is, like an ancestor from which all
> things come.
>
> It blunts sharpness, resolves tangles;
> It tempers light, subdues turmoil.
>
> A deep pool it is, never to run dry!
> Whose offspring it may be I do not know:
> It is like a preface to God.[19]

Tao as nature includes everything. There is nothing excluded from Tao. But what is this nature that penetrates and embraces everything? "The *Tao* principle," said Lao Tzu, "is what happens of itself [*tzu-jan*]."[20] *Tzu-jan*, "that which happens of itself," may be translated as spontaneity. By describing nature as *tzu-jan*, Lao Tzu tries to show that everything grows and operates on its own or as quoted in Zenrin Kushu: "(As I) sit quietly, doing nothing, spring comes and grass grows of itself."[21] To Chuang Tzu, spontaneity is "flowing like water." It is shifting direction with varying conditions like water finding its own channel.

The Way is not something we can get onto nor achieve, find, or grasp. The known is not the Way. The Way is not known. Our problem is that we want to know, we want to find, we want to get there. We have this idea that by knowing, by finding, by getting there, life will be better, more peaceful, and more prosperous. So we strive for it. We go in search of this ultimate. We move, we quest, we strive, we push, we beg, we try and try and try. The harder we try to get where we want to be, the more being has a way of eluding us—just as a rainbow only glows at a distance. Chuang Tzu tells us that the Way is near. It is so near. It is too near. And we miss it. We miss it because we want to go far without really knowing that which is near. When asked, what is the Way? Taoist masters often reply, "A bird in the nest." "The water is flowing." The answer that does not seem to answer may be the true answer. Our society is filled with the different ways and methods to achieve, attain, find happiness, and succeed. We tell people how to be cool, slim, smart, successful, great, wonderful, and marvelous. Our society says, "If you want to be somebody in this life, be there. Get there. Keep moving. Strive for it. Push hard. Because what you have is not good enough. Get going. Because to remain where you are is to be a 'nobody.'" In contrast, Chuang Tzu tells us that the Way is near. The Way is very near.

Conventional ways of thinking ingrained in us by our society may only lead us further and further away. Instead, stay. Just stay. Silence has a way of teaching. In the silence of nothing, we may hear the voices of our souls and learn of our destiny. In the silence of nothing, we may find ourselves in the Way without having gone anywhere. There is nowhere to go to. The Way just is. What is the Way? The Beatles said it: "Here, there, and everywhere."

3. Nothing

無為

> *Hui Tzu said to Chuang Tzu, "There is a big tree in my yard. I named it shu. It is crooked and bumpy. You can't even try to measure it. Its branches are all twisted. If you leave it by the road, carpenters will not even consider cutting it down. Your words too are big and useless, rejected by the people." Chuang Tzu said, "You are distressed by this big useless tree. Why don't you plant it in no-man's land. You can lie down under it and sleep because its life will not be shortened by axes. It can't be harmed because if it is useless, it can't get hurt."*
>
> —CHUANG TZU

IN A PROFOUND SENSE, the invitation to the Way is an invitation to nothing. It invites us to empty constructs that we may have about reality and about the definition and direction of life.

Chuang Tzu tells the story of an ugly tree, the tree named *shu*. The point of the story is, "If it is useless, it can't get hurt." A client told me one day during a therapy session,

"I wake up in the morning wondering if I will be happy today." We love to divide life into good and bad, happy and sad. We feel the need to be in a category we label as great and wonderful. The thought of being in a place that is neither one nor the other is foreign to us. We cannot be in nothing. It is absurd. But hurt, Chuang Tzu tells us, is about that struggle to be something. If we were nothing, we would not feel hurt. What can we learn from nothing? In chapter 11 of the *Tao Te Ching,* Lao Tzu writes:

> We join spokes together in a wheel,
> but it is the center hole
> that makes the wagon move.
>
> We shape clay into a pot,
> but it is the emptiness inside
> that holds whatever we want.
>
> We hammer wood for a house,
> but it is the inner space
> that makes it livable.
>
> We work with being,
> but non-being is what we use.[1]

Our society has not given enough thought to the word "nothing," for our first inclination is to see "nothing" as negative. We say,

> "He is going to amount to nothing."
> "They have nothing in comparison to us."
> "We have nothing in common."
> "You are good for nothing."

Both Lao Tzu and Chuang Tzu invite us to look closely at "nothing" and realize its unexpected transforming power. It is the emptiness inside that makes a pot a pot. It is the inner space that makes a house a house. The word "nothing" is also used in a variety of ways. It refers to elements we designate as negative in life, such as sickness, pain, old age, pathology, abnormality, and death. Chuang Tzu uses many "deformed" characters in his writing to explore this concept of nothingness. The theologian Paul Tillich uses the term "nonbeing" in referring to these same aspects of life. There is a certain profoundness about nothing. But we miss it in the quest for something. The very first evil, as recorded in the Bible, is Lucifer not wanting to be Lucifer. Lucifer wanted to be something else. He wanted to be God. And Eve did not like her innocence. She wanted to know good and evil. At the end of the six days of creation, God said, "It is good." Then came the fall. Eve thought, "This is not good enough. I want to be something else," and ever since, we have been creating our own suffering and pain. We have been systematically manufacturing pain for ourselves. Unless we understand the meaning of salvation, we will be caught in the cycle of suffering, the web of our own creation.

An Ugly Tree

Hui Tzu told Chuang Tzu about a very ugly tree name *shu* that stood in his yard. It was so ugly that no one wanted to look at it. It was so ugly that not even the most unskilled carpenter would ever consider using it. Hui Tai was deeply bothered by this ugly tree because it was useless.

I once had a client who thought like Hui Tzu. His life,

as he perceived it, was like this ugly tree. He did not like it at all, so he did everything he could to escape from it. He was running away from himself, from what he considered an ugly home, an ugly relationship, and an ugly state of being. This ugliness permeated the way he felt and thought of himself. His only escape was to run away from the reality of his past, which he did by wearing cool pants and shirts, sporting an elegant watch, carrying a fancy cell phone, and driving a cool car. But no matter how hard he tried, he could not ignore the negative feelings he had about himself. He was trapped, caught in the web that had been created for him[2] and, in part, that he had created for himself.

My client was hurting because he thought his wife did not like who he was. She was not, in his opinion, supportive, but rather told him everything he ought to be that he was not. He hated it, perhaps because he believed so strongly in what she said. The pain that he struggled with was the pain of wanting to be anything but himself and wanting to rid himself of his history—his filth, his embarrassment, his shame, his abuse, his chaos.

Hui Tzu did not like the ugly tree. He could not accept it, neither could he embrace it. My client did not like his "ugliness" either. But Chuang Tzu's response was totally unexpected. He asked Hui Tzu, "Why be bothered with the ugliness of the tree?" He showed Hui Tzu that it was precisely because it was ugly that it could bring him comfort. He urged him to lie down under it and be protected from the burning heat; after all, it would never be cut down. Then he added a deeply profound insight: "If it is useless, it can't get hurt."

My client was trying to run away. It pained him to think of his ugly past. Carl Jung tells us that our psyche will not allow us to ignore and deny painful aspects of our lives. It will continue to call us to embrace the shadow. And until we embrace it, the pain will not go away.[3] This explains my client's exhaustion. He was running, but the shadow followed him. His shadow was trying to tell him, "It is not about running away. It is about returning." We cannot bury our history, our past, or our struggles. Our whole story has to be acknowledged—the good, the bad, and the ugly. This wholeness includes our history, stories, past, and struggles. My client's intense pain is indeed a voice calling him to return to the ugly tree and rest in its shadow because "if it is useless, it can't get hurt."

One day, as I was driving to a friend's place, I turned to my wife and asked her for directions. She gave them, but I did not listen very carefully, and as a result I had to ask her to repeat them again and again. She eventually became upset and accused me of being a bad listener. In response, I immediately became defensive because I liked to think of myself as a good listener. In my anger, my mind started to search for reasons to affirm my listening skills. The atmosphere was tense. Suddenly, the thought of Chuang Tzu and the ugly tree came to mind. "Maybe," I thought, "I really am not a very good listener. Maybe she's right." No sooner had I had those thoughts than the anger subsided and my defensiveness dissipated. I turned to my wife and teased her about my listening skills. She was not amused, but I learned that in the shade of an ugly tree, play becomes a possibility. "Be an ugly tree," Chuang Tzu urges us. Be liberated.

Empty Space

Another way of looking at the ugly tree metaphor is through the recognition of emptiness. You cannot hurt a space. You can pinch it, you can punch it, you can poke it, you can pry it, but you cannot hurt it. It cannot be rejected, ignored, cursed, or discriminated against for it knows no pain. In emptiness, nothing gets rejected, ignored, cursed, or abused.

When I teach, I often yearn for lively discussions, arguments, debates, and deep conversations. When it does not happen, I feel disappointed with my self. However, I have learned that my wants get in the way and remove safe space from the class environment. My wants clog the atmosphere. When there is no space, free movement is impossible. Each class has a life of its own. Students bring with them their spirits and their personality and therefore it is important to give students the space just to be. Each of us has a deep yearning for space, a space for who we are essentially, a space to explore without the restriction of standards, a space to reflect on the inner self without the unconscious condemnation of societal norms. When a being is bombarded by the "oughts," it can't grow naturally. It becomes alienated from itself. But once given the open space of nothingness, a being moves naturally and spontaneously toward growth.

Nonbeing

There is yet another nothingness that evokes a sense of profoundness in life—the threat of nonbeing. The awareness that life is indeed a movement toward death adds depth to the human quest for meaning by raising profound questions. My therapist told me that there is no authentic journey toward life until one is confronted with death. I learned this in a very personal way. Dying people know what to teach about life.

Dad

In many different ways, my dad was a typical cultural Confucian. He believed in bringing honor to the family, and would tell us, "Do not bring shame. Strive for success. Take care of the family." Although he came from a small town in China and lived in a run-down shop house in Chinatown, Bangkok, he was determined to succeed. And he did. Without completing high school, he taught himself English and accounting and finally became the president of the Thailand Adventist Mission. Success was important to him. Being respected was important. Being recognized and acknowledged was expected. Being morally upright was his primary duty.

In 1997, my dad was diagnosed with prostate cancer. The doctor performed surgery and told him that he could live another ten years. He was happy thinking of all the things he could do in ten years, but three years later he began to have severe pain. I took him to see a urologist who told him, "We found another type of tumor in your bladder. It is aggressive . . . very aggressive."

My dad asked for his opinion about what to do.

"You have three options," he said. "First, you can say, 'I've lived a good life and so I'm going to just let it be.' Second, you can use radiation and chemotherapy. Third, you can try radical surgery."

The fifteen minutes he spent in the clinic that day had

a profound impact on my dad's life for the following two months. Those fifteen minutes listening to the doctor's diagnosis changed everything. He thought about his diagnosis. He read about it. He talked to people about it. He cried about it. He got depressed over it. He searched for the answer. He searched for the best possible solution. He prayed and within his heart he experienced hope and despair, confirmation and desperation. Though the whole family provided support, that was not sufficient, for it was he who had to make the journey. A few days later, I observed symptoms of depression, and his pain just got deeper and deeper. He cried often. He bargained with God.

One month before he passed away, my sister took him to the emergency room because of the level of pain he was experiencing. The emergency room technicians took some X-rays and ran a couple of tests. Later, the doctor called us and said, "It looks very bad." We asked him how bad. He replied, "I give him three months. The cancer has spread to his bones and his kidney." A week later, we got together and told him that the cancer had spread. We saw his tears. His hands were shaking. My sister sat by him, resting her head on his lap, crying.

"Are you afraid?" she asked.

"No . . . I'm going to miss you very much. I'm worried about Mom."

"Don't worry, we will take care of her," we told him.

He sobbed harder and said, "It is not the same. . . . It is not the same."

At home, we watched him go through loss after loss. Every few days, he had to cope with another loss. It was hard, very hard.

On the morning of October 16, my mom called and said, "Dad asked for you three times already. Please hurry." I went, and found my dad was sitting at the dining room table. All the children and in-laws were sitting around the table. My dad's eyes were red. His mouth quivered. "What is happening?" I asked. They answered, "He does not know why he cannot walk, why he cannot help himself." We tried to explain to him that he had cancer. It was perhaps the most painful moment of our lives to watch him plunge into the depth of despair. I watched him struggle to find hope in hopelessness and meaning in the darkness of this abyss. He bowed his head and prayed. It was hard to make out what he was saying, but what we could make out will remain with me for a very long time. "God have mercy on me, have mercy on me. Give me strength to face this disease."

On October 22, 1999, I got a call at 4:30 in the morning. "Come quickly," my sister said. I rushed to my sister's house, walked into my dad's room, sat by his bed, held his hand, and watched him take his last breath.

Thoughts from a Dying Man

In *Being and Time,* Heidegger suggests that the recognition of being as being-toward-death leads to self-awareness and the need for self-authentication through conscience.[4] My dad did not have the time to authenticate his being nor the energy to make certain of the actualization of his self. He experienced Heidegger's *Being and Time* in the most existential way. He was depressed. He was weak. He was exhausted. He was beaten. Yet from this experience emerged one of the most significant theological shifts in his life. It was as if this depression had introduced him to the most profound nothingness, and by staring straight into this nothingness, he had come to a profound realization of the meaning of life.

I learned two very important lessons from my dad during the last couple of weeks of his life.

My dad had spent his whole life trying to tell being how it ought to be. He thought that being cheerful in the face of death was the Christian thing to do. Smiling in the face of tragedy was his interpretation of how people of faith behave. Only the strong and the faithful could do this, and he wanted to be one of them. But it did not happen the way he wanted it to. He could not smile, although he tried. Instead, his eyes teared up and his lips quivered. He was trying to tell his heart how to be a good Christian, but his heart had a different message. As friends stood by his bed and held his hands, he confessed, "I thought I ought to be strong. I thought I ought to smile and be cheerful. I thought I ought to be an example of faith and not let this fear affect me. I tried. I tried really hard. But I did not succeed. When I try to smile, I feel my tears. When I try to project courage, I am overwhelmed with fear. When I try to laugh, I cannot convince myself of the humor. I am afraid. I am sad. I am confused, and I have learned through this entire experience that it is all right. It is all right to be afraid, to feel sad, to worry and have faith in God at the same time." My dad was trying to teach life how to live, only to realize finally that life could not be taught. One lives when one learns to listen to life. In the face of nothingness, my dad taught me a profound lesson on life: life has a life of its own.

The second lesson I learned from my dad came a couple

of weeks before he passed away. One evening my brother and I were sitting at the dining table having a conversation with him. We said, "Dad, you have lived a very fruitful seventy-six years. What advice do you have for us?" My dad, wise man that he was, smiled and said, "Don't take yourselves so seriously." I thought about that statement for a long time, trying to understand in a practical sense what it means not to take myself so seriously. I recall one evening when my wife and I were reading great quotations from a book, not long after we got married. We came across one quotation that said, "You grow up when you learn to laugh at yourself." Having made many mistakes in life, I was eager to hear what my wife had to say about herself.

"Have you ever laughed at yourself?" I asked.

"Yes," came the reply, "at the thought of marrying you." And she laughed and laughed and laughed. I did not find that very amusing at first but perhaps this was what it meant to not take myself seriously.

"Don't take yourself so seriously." What had my dad learned in the face of nothing? Perhaps after spending seventy-some years of his life trying to perfect his Confucian aspirations, he learned that there was more to life than pursuing all the "oughts." That in the final analysis life is not about achieving success and respect, but about who one is. The mental, emotional, and physical energy spent on achieving recognition were not worth the effort because in the face of nothingness, nothing really counts except what you hold within your heart. "Not taking myself so seriously" is perhaps about coming to the awareness that I do not have to be the most important person in my family, at my workplace, or in the classroom. That everybody rejects everybody at some point and so it is all right to be rejected. That being ignored sometime is not all that bad. That everything I say is not all that clever. That I say stupid things and make mistakes.

In essence my dad was telling me, "It is liberating to be an ugly tree."[5] Being ugly frees us from engaging in the peripheral areas of life that construct an illusion of our identity and plunge us into the arena that really matters in life. It is the nothingness that frees us from the noisy world so we may hear voices from our hearts. "If you are ugly, you can't get hurt."

4. Nothing and the Journey of Ninety Thousand *Li*

無為

There is a bird named P'eng whose wings are like clouds filling up the sky. He flips his wings leaping into the air rising up as high as ninety thousand li *piercing through the clouds and mist.*

—CHUANG TZU

WHAT DOES "NOTHING" have to do with the journey of ninety thousand *li*?[1] Leaping ninety thousand *li* sounds like a lot of effort. Isn't Chuang Tzu all about doing nothing? The paradox in Chuang Tzu's story is its beauty. It is through nothing that one can finally leap ninety thousand *li*. It is through nondoing that nothing is left undone. Chuang Tzu tells an interesting story of a cook name Ting. Cook Ting was butchering an ox for Lord Wen-hui. "At every touch of his hand, every heave of his shoulder, every move of his feet, every thrust of his knee—zip! zoop! He slithered the knife along with a zing, and all was in perfect rhythm."[2] "What marvelous skills," said Lord Wen-hui. To this, Cook Ting replied:

> A good cook changes his knife once a year—because he cuts. A mediocre cook changes his knife once a month—because he hacks. I've had this knife of mine for nineteen years and I've cut up thousands of oxen with it, and yet the blade is as good as though it had just come from the grindstone. There are spaces between the joints, and the blade of the knife has really no thickness. If you insert what has no thickness into such spaces, then there's plenty of room—more than enough for the blade to play about in.[3]

The art of cutting up an ox depends on how well we actually know the ox. In the same way, how well do we know who we really are? How well do we know our very being? The art of living depends on our ability to allow ourselves to be caught in the flow of nature. But often our social environment is more concerned with conquering, dissecting, and manipulating nature. It fails to realize that nature has a life of its own. Nature moves and flows and directs its course. How can one both observe nature and flow in its course?

Once on a lunch break, I walked toward the department of nursing. Before I had entered the office, I caught sight of the secretary, who thought that she was all by herself. She had turned on Wild Cherry's "Play That Funky Music" and was dancing to it. I watched with amusement. Perhaps sensing that she was not alone, she looked up and froze. All the eloquent movements ceased at once. She was blushing with embarrassment, and I was disappointed. I was hoping she would say, "Siroj, come and dance with me."

She stopped dancing because she became self-conscious. She became self-conscious because my presence reminded her that an office is not a dance floor. She was reminded of what she ought and ought not to do as a secretary. The "oughts" and the "shoulds" stripped her of her spontaneity. All the standards and "ought-tos" in our society clog our minds and keep us from truly observing nature, from truly observing who we are. We are filled with theories about ourselves. We acquire all these theories from science and philosophy, from psychology and theology, from biology and pharmacology. We are so filled with "ologies" and "isms" that we are unable to see ourselves for who we are. It is only in the silence that we can see clearly.

I used to associate tightness in my neck with anxiety. So whenever I felt this tightness, I would ponder its cause, and my anxiety would escalate. A theory has a way of turning itself into reality. One day, I began to experience this tightness and it occurred to me, after reflecting on Chuang Tzu's writings, that this was just a physical sensation probably caused by lack of sleep or stress. It was no actual fear-causing event. Apparently I had been creating the causal relation in my head. Chuang Tzu's nothingness cleared a space for me to see more clearly. In that sacred space of silence, without any judgment based on my own personal theory, I was able to deconstruct the illusion of causation.

The Little Quail and Sung Jung-tzu

After hearing stories about the bird named P'eng who could leap ninety thousand *li*, the little quail laughed. "Where does he think he is going? My best and greatest leaps only measure ten to twelve yards." To this little quail, P'eng is an illusion, a fantasy. Chuang Tzu comments, "Such is the difference between big and little."[4] Comparing P'eng to Sung Jung-tzu, he continues:

> Therefore a man who has wisdom enough to fill one office effectively, good conduct enough to impress one community, virtue enough to please one ruler, or talent enough to be called into service in one state, has the same kind of self-pride as these little creatures. Sung Jung-tzu would certainly burst out laughing at such a man. The whole world could praise Sung Jung-tzu and it wouldn't make him exert himself; the whole world could condemn him and it wouldn't make him mope. He drew a clear line between the internal and the external, and recognized the boundaries of true glory and disgrace. But that was all. As far as the world went, he didn't fret and worry.[5]

The little quail does not understand what Sung Jung-tzu realizes in his heart, that "there is no self for the Perfect; no merit for the Holy; no fame for the Sage." The little quails could leap only twelve yards. There are many little quails leaping around a couple of yards, but this quail can leap twelve yards and all the other quails applaud its accomplishment. But it is still a quail and not P'eng. There are Buddhist quails that keep five precepts and yet remain ordinary quails. There are Buddhist quails that keep two hundred and fifty precepts and leap eight yards. Other quails applaud. There are Christian quails trying very hard not to sin and then there are other Christian quails that are building schools and hospitals and converting thousands. They leap many yards, leaping into fame. There are enterprising quails that run family businesses and every member has food on the table. There are other enterprising quails that make millions, leaping twelve financial yards. Clever quails indeed, but they are quails that strive for perfection within the reality they have constructed. Some leap four yards, some leap five yards, some leap twelve yards. But they are still quails. Within the reality of no-soul, they strive for no-self. Within the reality of heaven, they strive for redemption. Within the reality of the material world, they strive for accumulation. Within the reality that they have created, they leap a couple of yards. But not so with P'eng. The secretary wanted to be more perfect and protect her reputation. Her feet suddenly had no rhythm, and her dancing ceased.

Chuang Tzu invites us to dance, to release the spirit from the artificial standard that has been imposed on being. Before you can leap and dance, the dance floor has to be cleared. The little quail is learning all the right steps because he is driven by fame, by good conduct. Sung Jung-tzu can leap ninety thousand *li* because there are no right steps. His heart is free to listen to the rhythm of his body. There is no right move except his move, no right steps except his steps. The dance floor is empty. The body must now be its own choreographer.

Ninety Thousand *Li*

Now that the dance floor is empty, what does it mean to leap ninety thousand *li*? P'eng can leap ninety thousand *li*. His back is as big as Mount T'ai, and his wings are like clouds in the sky. Flapping his wings, he leaps ninety thousand *li*. It is the empty space that helps him fly. When a house is full, a bird can't fly. A quail's world is filled up to the top with all the "oughts" and "shoulds." A quail's world is filled with an interpretation of reality of what it means to be a "quail." A quail's world is filled with artificial causal relations. That is why this little quail can only leap ten to twelve yards. The house is full. But not for P'eng.

We often interpret ninety thousand *li* as climbing the highest mountain, diving into the deepest ocean, fighting the fiercest enemy, and running the fastest race. There are people who think big, make discoveries, earn big money, and appear on big screens. They create the reality, strive for its "ought," and perfect their destiny in the path they have created. But, according to Chuang Tzu, these individuals only leap twelve yards because they cannot go beyond what their thoughts have created. Either they have achieved only what they believe to be success, or they have failed to achieve what they believe is success. But have they really achieved or failed? Who is to define what they have done? One person's failure may be another person's achievement. A loser in one place may be a winner in another geographical location. Who decides?

This is why these people are quails, but P'eng leaps. P'eng leaps because P'eng is not caught in the "this" and the "that." He is not affected by fame or applause. He is not hurt by rejection or condemnation. He is free to play. The dance floor is clear. The room is empty. He can leap and fall, sit and swing, dance and sing. And in this play he is able to listen to the rhythm of his own being, the rhythm that speaks of meaning. He becomes a butterfly flittering, fluttering. Or in Kuang-ming Wu's description:

> This man roams boundlessly within the universe. He is beyond us, not because he is above us but because he is at home everywhere among us, unhampered even by his self-concern (he has no self), his evaluation (no merit), his fame (no name). He roams (*yu*) in darkness and among the twigs, in government offices and in the field, in the wind and in calm lakes. He tarries wherever he happens to be, and the place is no longer big or small, far or near—it just is.[6]

This ninety thousand *li* is the ability to leap and roam freely, not being bound by the rules of one's creation or the games of one's society. For P'eng, to be good is not to be thought of as good. To be bad is not to be thought of as bad. To succeed is not to be compared to another's success and to fail is not something that can be told. Fame or shame is a question of definition. It is an obsession of those who are not satisfied with the "is." It belongs to the "this" and the "that." P'eng knows better. The "this" is actually the "that." Shame can be fame and fame can be shame. P'eng is affected by neither. "He is beyond us, not because he is above us but because he is at home everywhere among us."[7]

Play

"At home everywhere among us" evokes a sense of rest and authenticity. Indeed, life is a journey back to oneself.

It is returning home to who we are as a person. It is tracing the inner flow of the persons we are and allowing this flow to direct our lives rather than allowing a cognitive construction to determine life's course. This does not in any way suggest that we should abandon the role of cognition. Rather, it places cognition in service to life. The mind cannot tell life how to live because of its limitations, because life is beyond mind's ability to comprehend. But the mind is a wonderful instrument, essential and necessary, that facilitates life through its ability to organize.

How does one return to oneself? Psychoanalyst D. W. Winnicott introduces us to the importance of play in the soul's journey. Commenting on Winnicott's concept of play, Ann Ulanov, professor of psychiatry and religion, states, "The purpose of playing, aside from the sheer fun of it, amounts to finding and creating oneself and bringing alive the symbols that picture both a reality beyond the self and our experiences of uniting with it."[8] Play is the place of self-discovery. Play brings out the self as it is.

> The space of playing offers us rest from the daunting ego-task of trying to keep together outward reality and inward wishes and hopes. In the spaces in between, we take time off; we meander happily. We need not reconcile these opposites or hold them in tension. Here we can relax, not needing to achieve performance or purpose. . . . We do not, at this moment, have to hold up the world; we can let the pilot fly the plane.[9]

Play is possible when there is space. Without space, there is no play. Space is that place in between. A driven self finds itself in its striving toward the "ought." It is discontented with the "is." Space is the in-between place where one is given the freedom to just be without the demands of the "ought." A teenager no longer has to be cool; a scholar no longer has to be clever; a priest can admit his mistakes; a housewife can relax in untidiness. Ulanov's *Finding Space* helps me realize that the depth of one's psyche and the reality of one's self, which are often caught in the illusion of one's own creation, can only be actualized in the sacredness of space. Perhaps this helps to explain salvation by grace because grace is space. Space embraces. Without space, how can one be saved when it is hard to even realize what it is that needs saving? Being saved is being liberated from the illusion that one creates for one's self and thus, one's suffering. This space, Winnicott writes, "can be looked upon as sacred to the individual in that it is here that the individual experiences creative living."[10]

Space

Being liberated is not a cognitive exercise. It is not a mere realization of the societal aspiration. It must rather be in one's soul, one's heart. How can one arrive? This very question negates itself. In order to arrive, one presupposes a place to be or not to be, a good self or a bad self. To arrive is to miss the point. The radicalness of Chuang Tzu's teaching is precisely its invitation to rest. It is the call to be in the midst of dirt, mud, heat, rain, flowers, rocks, blue sky, and stormy sea. It is a call to rest under that ugly tree.

At the existential level, the self comes to recognize the double negatives in the process. In the first level of emptiness, one envisions oneself as being in a state of emptiness where the self recognizes the illusions of social constructions seeking to define the self. One recognizes that in emptiness, pain is removed and the self's spontaneity reemerges. But Chuang Tzu is more radical and perhaps even more in tune with the soul when his P'eng travels to the southern darkness. This is the second and a very essential negation. P'eng's ability to leap and roam freely emerges from this existential recognition of this second negative. The problem is that we do not see any light in this darkness. Kuang-ming Wu has profoundly explained this human dilemma:

> Sadly we do not know the night; we do not even like it. We despise its depths and mysteries. We do not feel our way in the night any more, but rob and probe it with flashlights of reason, senses, and tools, and laugh at those night-fumblers. We are cicadas and small doves, having lost a perspective of the starry night. We do not let the luring silence of darkness envelop us, as the Fish and the Bird did. We see darkness only as a metaphor for the absence of life, and forget that fish live there. We lose ourselves in the luminous shallows of clarity. We laugh nervously; we criticize endlessly. We think we know, and lose our refuge from the machinery of clarity. We think we can afford to lose the poetry of the fish, now that we take darkness to be mere nuisance.[11]

The emptiness here is the emptiness of the second negative, the darkness as constructed by the society that we have internalized in our hearts. It is the internalization that took place when we were named "misfit," "ignorant," "pathological," "codependent," and "failure." These stubborn feelings do not just go simply by realizing the illusory categories we use to define ourselves. Instead, the soul has to be caught up in the Way. The Way is that existential neutralization of the internalized negatives. The second negative is the power to stay in the darkness of the deep. It is the courage to remain within the discomfort one may feel, in the lack of spontaneity, in the pain of rejection. It is the sustaining power to rest under the ugly tree of jealousy, frustration, fear, and anxiety. Grace is the power that sustains, embraces, and holds a person within these negatives and through this act of embracing, redefines existential feelings, neutralizing them as neither "this" nor "that."

So the second negative is our ability to sit in it and name it, to feel the fear and describe the anxiety without naming it bad. And in this holding, a person can roam

> in darkness and among the twigs, in government offices and in the field, in the wind and in calm lakes. He tarries wherever he happens to be, and the place is no longer big or small, far or near—it just is. Nothing is either dark or in daylight, fantastic or trivial—it is just home. This is true transcendence, going beyond both the ordinary and the extraordinary.[12]

In this embracing is true leaping and roaming, the beginning of the ninety thousand *li*. In this "double negative," nothing is left to be negated. One can leap and roam in the southern darkness as one finally finds rest in the restlessness itself under an ugly tree.

Kuang-ming Wu writes, "Reverse your perspective; see the other side. Negate what you negated. Then you will see that [a negated twice becomes a rendered] flexible, cautious, and alive. In this manner, the very meaning structure of a notion comes alive, soaring and roaming."[13]

Psychiatrist Gerald May describes individuals who leap and roam:

> In a factory in a small Michigan town, I once came upon a woman whose eyes were so clear that I could not help but feel awed in her presence. She seemed not to know this, and only smiled gently at me. On a Pennsylvania farm, an old grandfather laughed lovingly as I spoke of understanding life. He twinkled, but said no words in response to me. Instead, he invited me to help with the milking of the cows. A suburban housewife heard me discussing the difficulties of being immediately aware. "Why is it so hard," she said, "when you are?"
>
> There are people like this everywhere. They simply have no great reason to announce themselves. They have no need to write, speak, teach or learn about awareness or being. Because they simply are, and their simple being says more than words ever could. . . . They live as best they can and accept their being at that. They do not try to do more than their best. Their behavior is responsible, but they assume neither credit nor blame. There is no need for them to try to live, for they are immersed in the process of living.[14]

5. Do Nothing

無為

What ordinary people do and what they find happiness in—
I don't know whether such happiness is in the end really
happiness or not. I look at what ordinary people find happiness
in, what they all make a mad dash for, racing around as
though they couldn't stop—they all say they're happy with it.
I'm not happy with it and I'm not unhappy with it.
In the end is there really happiness or isn't there?
I take inaction to be true happiness, but ordinary people
think it is a bitter thing. I say: the highest happiness has
no happiness, the highest praise has no praise. The world
can't decide what is right and what is wrong. And yet
inaction can decide this. . . . I say, Heaven and earth
do nothing and there is nothing that is not done.

—Chuang Tzu

Life is a journey into the indivisible "is." What is, just is. Perhaps what we need in our life and spirituality is to bring our busy "doing-something" to a stop and gather sufficient courage to just do nothing. But how do we "do nothing" psychologically, spiritually, and existentially?

> True perfection seems imperfect,
> yet it is perfectly itself.
> True fullness seems empty,
> yet it is fully present.
>
> True straightness seems crooked.
> True wisdom seems foolish.
> True art seems artless.
>
> The Master allows things to happen.
> She shapes events as they come.
> She steps out of the way
> and lets the *Tao* speak for itself.[1]

Personal Journey

I came to realize the need to stop through my existential agony. Not that I wanted to stop; I had to. My entire body and my mind were caught in a web of chaos and confusion. This is my story.

Growing up with two older sisters who did pretty well in school, I thought that perhaps, since we shared the same gene pool, school would be easy for me. However, my first report card showed that I ranked thirty-second in a class of only thirty-two students. I did not even know at the time just how badly I had done until it was explained to me that in ranking, bigger does not necessarily mean better. School was always a struggle for me. People like to think that boys don't do well in school but that instead they excel athletically. I wanted to think so, but that wasn't the case. I joined a basketball team but never had a chance to compete except on the day they could not find enough players. I felt like a fool running around the court, not being able to catch the ball. Humiliation had a profound effect on my personal identity and self-esteem.

One afternoon my oldest sister asked if I wanted to compete in a race. I immediately shook my head, but she was most persuasive. "Let's have a blind race. We'll close our eyes and run as fast as possible." It sounds stupid now, but back then it was very appealing. Here, I thought, was my chance to win at something. The race was on. My oldest sister, who had proposed the idea, volunteered herself as referee. When she shouted "go," my other sister ran cautiously, but caution was nowhere in my consciousness. I had to win, and so with my eyes tightly shut I ran as fast as I could. Did I win? I did not think there would be any obstacles, but there was an obstacle: a cement pillar at the finish line. I did not finish the race, but I did see many stars. This experience became a metaphor for my life for many years to come.

I did not like who I was. I did not like how I felt about myself. Throughout my teenage years, all I aspired to do was please my friends. I was always trying to fit in, always trying and never quite managing. This way of living life extended for me beyond my teenage years into my adult life. Eventually I realized that my life revolved around running and searching for a self—a self that was smarter, more successful, and more charming. Before long, though, valuation turned into depletion and finally major depression.

It was at this time that my soul was able to speak to me and I slowly came to a stop. In the midst of this immobility was nothingness, painful darkness. Then God said, "Let there be light."

> Woodworker Ch'ing was carving wood for a bellstand. When the bellstand was completed, all who saw it were as amazed as though they were seeing the work of a spiritual being. The Marquis of Lu went to see it and inquired of the woodworker, saying, "With what art have you made this?"
>
> "Your subject is merely a workman," was the reply. "What art could I possess? However, there is one thing. When I am getting ready to make a bellstand, I dare not waste any of my energy, so it is necessary to fast in order to calm my mind. After fasting for three days, I no longer presume to harbor any thoughts of congratulations and rewards, of rank and salary. After fasting for five days, I no longer presume to harbor any thoughts of censure or praise, of skill or clumsiness. After fasting for seven days, I abruptly forget that I have four limbs and a body. At that time, I have no thought of public affairs or the court. My skill is concentrated and all external distractions disappear. Only then do I enter the mountain forest and observe the heavenly nature of the trees till I find one of ultimate form. Only after the completed bellstand manifests itself to me do I set my hand to the work. Otherwise, I give up. This

> is heaven joined to heaven. This is what makes one suspect that my instruments were made by a spiritual being."[2]

In a painful way I was led to this experience of nothingness. Gradually this nothing took on a profound meaning. I started to see the "heavenly nature of the trees." Depression spoke to my soul. Through it, I came to realize that I needed to stop running and stop searching for myself. I learned that to search for the self elsewhere is to deplete one's self. The self is here—right here—and what one needs to do is to stop.

Pathology and the Bellstand

Taking this concept a step further, Chuang Tzu has persuasively convinced me that nature, even in its pathological form, may be heavenly ordained.

In *Listening to Prozac,* Peter Kramer recounts the story of a woman named Allison and her continual struggle with low self-esteem. She felt ugly, socially awkward, and dumb. She often compared herself to one of her cousins who always seemed better than her in every way. After four months of Prozac, Allison went to visit her cousin.

> She had always wanted red hair and green eyes like this cousin; Alison had blond hair and blue eyes, but somehow the family had made her feel this coloring was second best. As a gradeschooler, Allison ate carrots and beets in the hopes that her hair would turn red. She made

> over her dolls in the cousin's image. Over the years, everything about this cousin had been better: her native intelligence, the college she went to, her field of study, the man she married, the part of the country she lived in. And, of course, the cousin was taller and thinner.
>
> But this time when she visited the cousin, Allison no longer felt like the dumb one: "So she went to a better college. What does she do with it? She sits home and reads women's magazines. I would never trade my children for her children." The two went grocery shopping, and the cousin tried to convince Allison that sea scallops were better than bay scallops. "I almost believed her—any other time I would have believed anything she said. This time I said, 'Whatever do you mean?' What I meant was, 'I am not an ugly idiot.' And then I noticed I was taller than she was—and I had been for thirty years."[3]

Allison felt more love and appreciated. She no longer struggled with her sensitivity toward rejection. Her life took on a different meaning because of Prozac.

I once learned from a psychiatrist, at a seminar on mental health, that Serotonin Reuptake Inhibitors (SSRI) have the added feature of being able to remove shyness. Before I came to the United States, I received *Scope*, a magazine published by Loma Linda University. On the front cover of one issue, I clearly remember the picture of a student in the nursing department receiving her diploma. Looking at the picture, I was very impressed because the student seemed to be very excited and expressive as she waved her diploma in the air saying, "Yea." Staring at the picture, I thought to myself, "This is how I want to be. I want to be expressive."

I'm a shy person, a very shy person. I feel nervous when I'm in a big group. I can't talk when I'm sitting with many people. When people greet me, I get nervous and sometimes say the wrong thing. When I see someone walking toward me, I normally try to think ahead about what to say. The problem, though, is that when I'm asked a different question, I still reply with the pre-prepared answer.

"How is your family?" "Oh, I'm fine."

"Where are you going?" "I've eaten already."

Is it so bad to be mad? Is it so bad to be ordinary, anxious, or shy? Yes and no. It was painful, and yet out of this experience of pain came many wonderful life-changing perspectives. My shyness, my anxiety, and depression contributed in a significant way to how I have come to reconfigure reality and discover shades of meaning in my life. These "pathologies" have granted me the permission to descend into the very depths of my soul.

I once saw a lady wearing a t-shirt that read, "I'm co-dependent and I love it." I'm not asking anyone to go crazy and be mad, but I am suggesting that that which has been given to us is sacred. Our weakness, our deficiency, our pathology can be our calling as well.

Eleanor Roosevelt was a shy and awkward child. She recounted how as a little girl she constantly craved recognition and love, and she would frequently fantasize about things. Often a fantasy is called an escape, but for some it is a calling. "I grew up with a fear of insanity," she wrote. By the time she was five, she became difficult. She was stubborn, sullen, spiteful, and sour. "She lied; she stole; she threw antisocial tantrums in company. She was taught and subdued by a tutor, whom she 'hated for years.'"[4] Before she turned nine, she lost her playboy father, her younger brother, and a mother who never liked her. Today a case similar to that of Eleanor Roosevelt would require extended psychotherapy. A case conference would be called, and family dynamics analyzed, including experimentation with various types of psychotropic medication to reduce the strength and frequency of her images and ease the mind of its obsession, "thereby proving by circular reasoning that what it had eliminated was indeed disease."[5] But this did not happen in Mrs. Roosevelt's life. Instead, for her, "imagination acted as teacher, giving instruction for the large ministering tasks of caring for the welfare of a complex family, of a crippled husband, of the state of New York as the governor's wife, the United States as its First Lady, and even of the United Nations."[6] Her fantasies became her calling. Through them, she became devoted to the underprivileged of all races and nations. Through them, she gave her life to the welfare of others.

I love those words on the t-shirt, "I'm co-dependent and I love it." The crosses we carry, our pathologies, our weaknesses, and our deficiencies may in the end prove to be our greatest gifts for humanity. Prozac is good, Zoloft is good, and Paxil is good, and yet we also need never to forget the sacredness of our lives, the sacredness of everything that makes us the person that we are. This, according to Chuang Tzu, is the principle of heaven and earth. Looking at our theory-driven society, Chuang Tzu might have responded, "Heaven gave you a body and you use this body trying to distinguish between 'hard' and 'white.'"[7]

Perhaps life invites us to look deeper and see the "bell-stand" in the tree that others may call ugly, unfit, and useless. Life invites us to resist others' labels, norms, and standards and to find within ourselves those heavenly forms no matter what they may be. In finding them, we create space for the natural to emerge. In our natural tendency to strive, to struggle, and to fight, we hear Chuang Tzu's concern being echoed through the words of psychiatrist Gerald May, "One need do nothing, nothing at all."[8]

Practical Nondoing

The practice of nondoing itself is a challenge. In a sense, one needs to realize that this nothing is really nothing. It is not nothing for something. It is nothing for nothing. I learned this the hard way, and I am still learning. I am naturally an anxious person and do not know how else to be. If things do not go the way I imagine them to be, my anxiety escalates. This anxiety plays itself out vividly in the classroom. I think deep and long, searching for something profound to share in class. In delivering my lectures, I long to mesmerize the class with my depth, creating magic for the moment. When they respond with yawns or blank stares, my anxiety heightens, my confidence dissipates, and the downward spiral begins.

Chuang Tzu helps me realize the false dichotomy in these expectations. The standards that I set for myself are my own creation. The students' evaluations are theirs. Educational measurement changes over time. It does not emerge from the natural. Therefore, measurements do not define who I am, and they do not determine my value as a person. In Chuang Tzu I found liberation. I was liberated to be me, to be nonanxious, to realize that success and failure are human creations. This liberation comes with a sense of peace and inner comfort. The amazing thing is that the more I relax, the better I teach, because the less anxious I am, the better my students respond. Things began to get better, and I began to like the outcome. However, trying to be less anxious for a better outcome is not right either, because the outcome itself creates the anxiety. J. Krishnamurti states, "A problem exists only in the search for a result; and the problem ceases if there is no search for a result."[9] In another lecture, he teaches:

> So what is important is to understand why the mind is disturbed. What is this disturbance? Basically, fundamentally, does it not come about when there is this constant urge to be something, the desire for a result, the desire for self-improvement, the desire to achieve a certain noble action? As long as one is competitive, ambitious, there must be disturbance, there must be conflict.[0]

Perhaps this is where the profound nothingness comes in. This is the double negatives. Perhaps this is where one really needs to learn to stop. It is not possible to do nothing in order to get something out of it, because then, it defeats its purpose. It has to be nothing for nothing. It is not giving so that we may receive, loving so that we may be loved, honoring so that we may be honored, working hard so that we may get a raise. It is nothing for nothing, which means that our actions do not emerge from the desire to improve the beings that we are but from the acceptance of what is.

A number of years ago my former professor told me that he no longer experienced dichotomy in his life. Back then, I did not really know what he meant. With the help of Chuang Tzu, I am beginning to understand. We create many false dichotomies for ourselves. Dietrich Bonhoeffer offers an insight into this problem of dichotomy. In the very opening sentence of his book *Ethics,* he suggests that thinking in terms of right and wrong needs to be overcome because it presupposes our disconnection with God, the very source of life.[11]

Perhaps in the struggle with our anxiety and discomfort (the drive to strive for something), Chuang Tzu is begging us just to stop and sit. Life is not always high and exciting. There are low places and emptiness at times. It is just the natural flow of life. As we sit silently in our own anxiety and our discomfort, we learn to integrate the natural flow of life. We learn to listen to life instead of trying to tell life how to live. Life has a life of its own, and listening is that calling. The only way to listen is to learn to stop and to sit in the sense of discomfort, anxiety, and emptiness. Only in the space of nothingness can the soul find its place, its calling.

Observing Life

Listening to life presupposes that life is a living entity. It moves, it grows, it prospers. Sitting in the shades, it moves toward light. Facing the storm, it sinks its roots deep in the soil. One would be wise to learn to listen to life, to learn to observe life. Gerald May calls this process the art of awareness:

> The importance of awareness then is not so that we can better control ourselves. It is not so that we can analyze and interpret our minds or bodies or the world around us. To use awareness as a tool for self-manipulation only leads to treachery. Awareness is a space giver. An open window, letting the fresh air in. It unties the knots and loosens the tension. Awareness with full acceptance is like pure sunlight shining into a cellar, making it possible for healing to happen and growth to take place. One has to do nothing with it.[12]

In observing, we learn that often the pain we experience is related to the identity we give to ourselves. "He thinks I'm stupid, but I'm not stupid." "She thinks I'm lazy, but I'm not lazy." "They ignore me." "They discriminate against me." If there is no "I," what "they" think does not really matter. If there is no "me," discrimination cannot hurt, because hurt comes from believing that I'm not stupid nor lazy, that I'm important because I'm an ethnic minority. We've come to identify ourselves through the socialization process. But is this me that I cling to really me? To Chuang Tzu, this is nothing but "three in the morning."[13] Often this thing we identify as "me" is socially constructed. One can be pretty in one culture and ugly in another. One may be smart in one community and overbearing in another. One can be energetic in one family and annoying in another. Chuang Tzu states the "this" is the "that" and the "that" is the "this." When we are able to sit back and observe life, we come to the realization that the "me" transcends the way we have normally internalized ourselves. What we have internalized and the pain we have been experiencing are caused by created categories of those who are not happy with the "this as is." It is indeed their discomfort with their "isness" that results in such proliferation of "oughts" and "shoulds." Through observation, one learns of the thoughts, emotions, tensions, and sensations that arise and gradually fade away. One learns to notice what is as things come and go without rushing to name them as "me." Observing is suspending judgment and analysis, permitting the self to notice things arising, things vanishing, the tension, the obsession, the pleasure, the excitement, and trusting that life knows how to grow and heal.

Describing the process of observation, Richard Young writes:

> If I'm on a runaway train and don't know it, then that train is my only reality and I'm in big trouble. I can't get off because there's no "off" to get to. But when I finally realize I'm riding on an

> endless train of conditioned thoughts that constantly create painful experiences, I have taken my first steps on the path of mindfulness. And if I am learning to stand at the crossing watching the cars go by and noticing what each contains without clinging to some or averting my gaze from others, then I am free. Or at least I'm beginning to taste freedom.[14]

Krishnamurti calls this process meditation. "Meditation is to be aware of thought, of feeling, never to correct it, never to say it is right or wrong, never to justify it, but just to watch it and move with it."[15] Awareness does not only help free us from misrepresentation of the self. Awareness itself, without any attempt to fix and judge, is able to dissolve the power of pain in one's life. In his 1953 lecture in London, Krishnamurti states: "To be radically free from fear is to be aware of fear and to leave it alone, without any judgement, without trying to do anything about it. Just to know that there is fear and to be quiet, brings about a fundamental revolution in which fear has no longer any place."[16] Observe and do nothing about it. To Krishnamurti, to observe in quietness is the key to conquering pain. But one must understand that in the last analysis, it has no aim of conquering anything. One does nothing for nothing, the nothing of a thousand *li*.

Reflecting on the art of doing nothing reminds me of the ending of Disney's *Toy Story* when Buzz Lightyear finally realizes that he is just a toy and not a space hero: "Buzz realized that Andy loved him. Now he knew what it meant to be a toy. It was even better than being a space hero."[17]

6. The Nothing of Love and the Love of Nothing

Fish live in water and thrive, but if men tried to live in water they would die. Creatures differ because they have different likes and dislikes. Therefore the former sages never required the same ability from all creatures or made them all do the same thing. Names should stop when they have expressed reality, concepts of right should be founded on what is suitable.

—CHUANG TZU

ALTHOUGH CHUANG TZU does not speak much of love directly, many of his teachings about paradox and nothingness can be applied to the concept of love. Love can make us laugh. Love can make us cry. It is like wasabi. It can hurt and yet one can't live without it.

When I was young, I never had any luck with the girls in my school. I used to observe myself in the mirror and think I was a combination of Jet Li and Chow Yang Fat. However, none of the girls in my class shared my opinion, except once when I was in seventh grade and there was a girl named Anna. She was tall, slim, and wealthy. She sent me roses and a valentine card, called me constantly on the phone and told me about her eight servants, ten-bedroom house, and personal chauffeur. However, I felt no chemistry with her, and I did not pursue the relationship. Now, some thirty years later, I regret that a little! With a ten-bedroom house, I would have had plenty of time to work on chemistry!

When I went to college in Singapore, I met a Chinese girl who was not rich. She did not have a personal chauffeur or a ten-bedroom house. She did not send me a valentine card. The first time I noticed her, she was playing basketball. She was wearing a blue t-shirt and white shorts. She was running around the basketball court. Just running. No one passed the basketball to her because she did not really know how to play. Occasionally, however, the basketball was passed to her, but she always missed. But even when she missed, she missed with charm. At the end of the game, I was sitting at the steps near the court, and I could not take my eyes off her. Her face was red. As I watched the sweat dripping down the curve of her cheeks, I thought, "Wow . . . I did not know there could be so much romance in perspiration." I was obsessed with her. I could not get her out of my mind. I told God, "If I don't marry this lady, I will die." Finally, I gathered enough courage and wrote her a little note: "Please meet me at the front of the cemetery at 4:30 p.m." At the college that we were attending, the most popular place for couples to go dating was the cemetery across from the campus. We walked to a quiet and romantic corner in the cemetery, and, sitting on Mr. Kim Yung Sun, 1910 to 1957, I confessed my love to her. Mr. Kim was my witness, and he was dead serious.

Love is so intoxicating. And twenty-some years after my romantic confession before Mr. Kim, I have learned many great lessons about love. I have learned that life yearns for love. Its longing is existential, it is ontological. It is as instinctive as a plant reaching for the light. Where there is no love, there is no life. The apostle Paul writes, "But the greatest of these is love."

We go to work. Make tough decisions. Provide solutions. Give good advice. Increase production. Achieve recognition. But, when we return home, there is a little child in us longing to be touched, to be held, to be comforted, to be affirmed. There is a longing for a smile, a squeeze on the shoulder, a place of acceptance, and a word of comfort. We need love. We really need love. Yet it is probably the rarest and most difficult to define of human commodities. It is a mystery that millions have braved attempts at explaining, but it moves on, unchanged with the times and untouched by human intellect. It is in the tears of a little child, in a cup of cold water offered to others, in a smile. In its presence, we become speechless. Words fail as does any other construct. It transcends every human attempt to possess. Love is. It is there. It is not something we can have as in an object: it just is. It has a life apart from what we may think or do. Through disappointment, pain, brokenness, disillusionment, abuse, and injustice in human society, love remains. If we have not been touched by love at some level in our lives, perhaps it is because we do not allow love to be love. We hold it within our definition. We control it through our persuasion. We search with a preconceived conceptualization. We yearn to be touched by love—but only with the love we have predefined. Although Chuang Tzu has not written much on the topic, I'm persuaded that he would have invited us to begin our exploration with nothing, with the nothing of love.

Nothing of Love

Perhaps the primary step in the journey of love is that profound nothingness. According to Chuang Tzu, pain is often the result of our constructs. We create and we define, and when we do not experience love in accord with our definitions, we become desperate. We symbolically fight and kick and scream for something that may have already been present in our lives. But the fight goes on because we are blinded by our own constructs.

Once while in college I had a fever. In my family, sick people are treated really well, and I was used to receiving a lot of attention when I was ill. My parents would ask, "What would you like to eat?" or "What can I get for you?" Even now that I'm grown, they treat me this way. Once, as an adult, I was sick and my dad came to visit. He thought that my sickness had to do with my financial stress, so before leaving, he slipped $200 into my hand. At that moment, I wished I could get sick more often!

So when I got sick that day in college, I told a friend first thing in the morning to please inform my girlfriend of my illness as soon as possible. I visualized her rushing to my room to take care of me. I waited and waited. Finally, during her lunch break she came to my room, looked me over, and said, "You're not that sick."

"I am," I said, trying to be as persuasive as possible.

She looked around the room, saw a tray of food, and asked, "Why aren't you eating?"

"I'm too sick to eat," I told her.

So she grabbed the tray of food and began eating, working her way down to the last vegetable stem. Then she turned and said, "You'd better get well soon."

I remember thinking to myself, "How mean! How can she do this to me? I'm sick!"

I later learned that in her family, everyone is expected to carry on normal everyday duties when they get sick. A person can get out of duties only when the sickness is severe. So there I was feeling unloved, but not because there was no love. I missed her love because I was looking for the kind of love as defined by my little family's subculture. Looking for love through a predefined lens creates pain for us. Listening to young people talk about love and dating in American culture, I have learned that if there are no kisses during a couple's first few dates, something isn't right. However, a Hong Kong girl who just got married told me, "My first kiss was a year after we started dating." I do not think there is any less love in Hong Kong, but there might be quite a bit of confusion if a Hong Kong girl were to go on a date with an American boy.

The construct of love is not only culturally influenced; one's perception of love is also influenced by one's temperament, family background, and personal experience.

Perhaps the very first step in the quest for love is the willingness to empty our constructs of love. Speaking of emptiness, Chuang Tzu writes, "Look at this window: it is nothing but a hole in the wall, but because of it the whole room is full of light."[1]

The second step, in the spirit of Chuang Tzu, is probably to learn to listen to love, the love that lies within our soul. In listening, it is essential to clear space so that the materials of the soul may emerge. Oftentimes we have a certain understanding of what love ought to be, and, as we align ourselves to that preunderstanding of love, we do not permit the very essence of ourselves to emerge. We were taught that love only wants the best for others, but there are times when we want to see the worst. We were taught that love does not covet, but occasionally we only want that which does not belong to us. Love forgives, but at the very same time it may desire to curse, using the worst words our vocabulary can offer. We were taught to tame the force of passion, yet the passion we name unacceptable lies hidden from our conscious mind and remains in our subconscious, showing itself in different faces and forms, through obsession and fantasy, desire and depression. Love cannot be tamed by the process of rationalization. It has its own determination and direction. It can't be captured in a frame. The only way to contain love is to recognize it, acknowledge it, and ruminate on it. We can't tell love how it ought to live within our souls. It is just there, operating on its very own mechanism. It is lofty yet instinctual. We can only observe, listen, and make the best decision. But listen we must. In the introduction to his book *Soul Mates: Honoring the Mysteries of Love and Relationship*, Thomas Moore describes our society as the "fix-it" society that sees human relationships as things that need to be managed using various instruments from experts in the field of marriage and family therapy such as systems, charts, and assessment tools to resolve complex human relationships. But to Moore the soul is not about fixing. It is about listening.

> Concerned about the soul, we don't ask why something has happened in a relationship, or how to make it better. Rather, we wonder about the soul's own purposes: "What is happening in the soul when we fall madly in love? What is the soul wanting in its fantasies of separation? What is this longing for deeper love, and why does it never seem to be satisfied?"[2]

In another place, Moore specifically invites us to explore the mysteries of the soul, since, from his perspective, marriage is not about a functioning family, many happy children, a healthy bank account, or a good retirement plan. The primary task of a marriage is "to evoke the soul's lover, to stir up this magical fantasy of marriage and to sustain it, thus serving the particular all-important myth that lies deep in the lover's heart and that supplies a profound need for meaning, fulfillment, and relatedness."[3] "One should rather," writes Moore, "protect and feed the deep fantasies that surround the other's imagination of love and marriage."[4]

What Moore has written regarding marriage applies, in a similar sense, to the experience of love in one's soul as well. The calling is to listen to the soul's language of love through various textures of sensation, emotion, thought, and fantasy.

Love of Nothing

We often think in terms of causal relations, and this natural tendency plays an essential role in human relationships. When I talk, people should listen. When I give, they should be thankful. When I ask, they should listen. When I educate, they should learn. When I am kind, I should receive kindness in return. When I love, there should be reciprocation. It is hard to act and think in a noncausal relation manner. When we care, we want to see improvement for those we care for. When we love, we want to see the fruit of our love. We want to know that our love matters. We want to see how love affects others. We want to feel a response to the love we offer. We want to love and be loved and know that love is the greatest of all because it makes us feel good about loving, it helps us to see others changing, and it makes the world a better place. But what if we do not see, feel, or realize all that we wish the power of love could alter in our lives? What if love is love, period? Could it be that love is the willingness to give the best that we have and let heaven handle the rest?

Leo Buscaglia recounts a story about a little prince who sat on the moon feeling bored as he listened to the rose boast about her beauty, her elegance, her charm, and her fragrance. The little prince decided to go visit the earth. While he was there, he came across a fox, a very wise fox who said to him, "Please tame me." The little fox went on to explain that the process of taming is like the process of forming a relationship, getting to know people, and learning to care. The little prince then said that he had to return to his place. "Indeed, when you do, I'm going to be very sad, I'm going to cry." The prince asked, "Why on earth would you want me to tame you if it is going to cause you pain?" And the fox said, "It's because of the color of the wheat fields." The fox explained:

> I do not eat bread. Wheat is of no use to me. The wheat fields have nothing to say to me. And that is sad. But you have hair that is the color of gold. Think how wonderful that will be when you have tamed me! The grain, which is also golden, will bring me back the thought of you. And I shall love to listen to the wind in the wheat.[5]

After the taming ritual, the fox asked him to go back and look at his rose again.

> "You are beautiful, but you are empty," the prince said. "One could not die for you. To be sure, an ordinary passerby would think that my rose looked just like you—the rose that belongs to me. But in herself alone she is more important than all the hundreds of you other roses: because it is she that I have watered; because it is she that I have put under the glass globe; because it is she that I have sheltered behind the screen; because it is for her that I have killed the caterpillars; because it is she that I had listened to, when she grumbled or boasted, or even sometimes when she said nothing. Because she is my rose."[6]

Love is like this little prince's investment in the rose—watering, pruning, and getting rid of caterpillars. It is the commitment that makes meaning for the lover. And love continues even when the petals start to fall and the leaves begin to wither. Love gives and it continues to give into nothingness. Taking this a step further, love provides space for another person even when this act of giving may in itself be painful, even when it may be hurtful. Love is holding on to someone even when one is being attacked, pushed, rejected, denied, and ridiculed. In *Finding Space: Winnicott, God, and Psychic Reality*, Ann Ulanov beautifully articulated the sacredness of such love:

> We destroy our projected object. But then, the object itself still stands there before us, existing in its own right, external to our creation of it and our projections upon it, surviving out of its own resilience and power. As Winnicott puts it: "The subject says to the object, 'I destroyed you,' and the object is there to receive the communication. From now on the subject says, 'Hullo object!' 'I destroyed you.' 'I love you.' 'You have value for me because of your survival of my destruction of you.'" Now we confront the object as other to us, as one who may bring to us real resources out of its own reality, one that may differ from and exceed the resources we ascribe to it in fantasy.[7]

Love is that ability to survive the intense quest, rejection, and even attack of the one we love. It is the ability to hold, regardless. Using the example of the mother-child relationship, Ulanov writes, "The mother survives our destroying our picture of her. She rebounds out of herself and her own resources, not because the child withholds his ruthless instinct. For there she stands, external, real, with him."[8] Hence in some strange way, love moves from nothing to nothing. And out of this nothingness comes the most meaningful existential decision that authenticates one's very existence—love.

7. Good for Nothing

無為

Right is not right; so is not so. If right were really right, it would differ so clearly from not right that there would be no need for argument. . . . Forget the years; forget distinctions. Leap into the boundless and make it your home!

—CHUANG TZU

If good may not really be all the good and bad is not as bad as it sounds, is Chuang Tzu promoting ethical relativism? Is there any basis for ethical decisions in his understanding of reality? Is there a place for moral decision? This, to me, is one of the most challenging aspects of Chuang Tzu's teaching. The following pages are my attempt to articulate the place of ethics in Chuang Tzu's writings.

A joke was told of three boys boasting about their fathers. The first said, "My dad is a doctor. I can get sick for nothing." The second competed: "Mine is better. He is a lawyer and I can get caught for nothing." The third boy joined in the conversation: "My dad is a pastor. I can be good for nothing." I would like to propose that this is exactly what Chuang Tzu is suggesting as a basis for ethical conducts: being good for nothing. From his perspective, what does it mean to be good for nothing?

The Problems

To Chuang Tzu, ethical and moral problems start when we do not pay attention to life and begin to discriminate between hard and white. By so doing, we impose artificiality onto reality, mechanize life, create chains of complexity, and perpetuate the process of dehumanization. If Chuang Tzu were to be asked, "What is good?" he probably would answer, "What is, is good." This answer would most likely be followed by strings of questions about its wisdom or the lack thereof. How is it possible for "what is" to be good? Discrimination, misappropriation, corruption, and abuse exist in our society. Are we to embrace them and say, "They are good"? Good questions deserve good answers. Clarity of thought, Chuang Tzu reminds us, should be our approach. People are people: they come in many sizes, shapes, forms, temperaments, intellectual capacities, and personalities. It is the fact of life. It is. But our dislike of what is leads us to prefer one over the other. Hence the adjective "good" is assigned to our preferences and thus begins the process of discrimination. We want to be rich, tall, slim, smart, cool, and attractive. We want power and control. This desire initiates the cycle that deteriorates human spirits. To achieve the category we have created for ourselves, we strive so we can feel good about ourselves.

We strive because we can no longer feel good about ourselves as we are. And we move on from needs, to wants, to greed. We move on from inner dissatisfaction to discrimination, corruption, and abuse. Clarity, says Chuang Tzu, is what we need. Would it not be true to say, the fewer categories we create, the less need there is to discriminate. When being cool is not so important, being a loser becomes less painful. When being recognized is not high on the priority list, being ignored isn't all that bad either. Categories create wants. Wants lead to greed. Imagine a society that is not obsessed with good looks, wealth, and the need to be perceived as successful. Such a society would contain less striving, less discrimination, and less want. Many of the problems we witness in our society as immoral or unethical often begin in discrimination and in dissatisfaction of what is.

The life of Nuan, a fourteen-year-old student from Roi Et Province in Thailand, tells the story of dissatisfaction that leads to discrimination and ultimately to dehumanization.

> Her parents are farmers whose bodies have borne the raging heat of the sun while planting rice in the field. Nuan recalled with fondness days when she used to play in the rice field: "We were poor but villagers were friendly and kind. They always extended hospitality to one another." Soon, through commercials and mass media, things began to change. Technology was introduced into the village in the name of progress and development. Villagers started competing

> with one another and comparing commodities. Women even compared dresses. To Nuan, this so-called development blinded their souls and perpetuated greed, especially in the case of her father. "He did not know how to be a dad anymore," she recalled.[1]

If the story had ended here, it may not have been so dehumanizing. But dissatisfaction has a way of destroying the very thing it wants. Through her dad's deceptive persuasion, Nuan was tricked into working in the sex trade in the red-light district in Bangkok. She was coerced to dance, use drugs, and "entertain" clients.

> For one year she was haunted by her father and sister, the two family members who gained from her pain, the two family members who could quantify commodities and compete with neighbors through the proceeds from her body. Sex was tolerable, but betrayal was more than this little girl could bear. She had a nervous breakdown, was hospitalized, and asked to quit her job. As she started to heal, her father came to persuade her to return to the go-go bar because "the income was much better."[2]

Nuan's story is the story of mass media defining "good" and perpetuating multiple layers of categories, making it difficult for farmers to remain satisfied with what they have and with who they are. Buffalos and bullock carts are now symbols of failure, of a lack of development. The dress code has changed, and beauty has been redefined. More glamorous symbols of success, honor, and worth have been introduced to the society, and they have caused farmers to thirst for a life that extends way beyond crops in the field. An innocent girl is sacrificed on an altar of prestige because "what is" is no longer good enough.

This is what Chuang Tzu sees—the forest and not the trees. The true problem is not just the "wrong" or evil that people engage in. Evil and immorality are symptoms of one's dissatisfaction with what is. People want more than what is. Chuang Tzu recognizes that Nuan's tragedy is a symptom of an idea. Her dad is a victim of ideas created by multimillion-dollar corporations flourishing around the globe trapped in their own creation of categories, the "this" and the "that," the "is" and the "ought." Eske Møllgaard, reflecting on Chuang Tzu's ethics, reminds us that unless we are in touch with our destiny and our nature before thinking about ordering the world, "the result will only be more violence."[3] Chuang Tzu understands that underlying these struggles and strivings are created categories, categories that emerge from dissatisfaction with what is.

How then should one go about life and deal with struggles and strivings? Chuang Tzu asks that we pursue nothing, that we become good for nothing. Here I explore three types of nothings: nothing in return, nothing in good and evil, and absolutely nothing.

Nothing in Return

Reflecting on the human tendency toward discrimination, Thomas Merton writes:

> As soon as man becomes aware of doing good and avoiding evil, he is no longer perfectly good. Ethical rationalization makes possible that schizoid division between words and acts, between thoughts and deeds, which finally reduces honest activity to complete helplessness, or else lays the way open for political or religious crooks to do all the evil they like in the name of "righteousness."[4]

Perhaps this understanding of the destructive power of discrimination is best understood in the context of Merton's translation of Chuang Tzu's "The Great and Venerable Teacher" which he entitled, "The Man of Tao."

> The man in whom Tao
> Acts without impediment
> Harms no other being
> By his actions
> Yet he does not know himself
> To be "kind," to be "gentle."
>
> The man in whom Tao
> Acts without impediment
> Does not bother with his own interests
> And does not despise
> Others who do.
> He does not struggle to make money
> And does not make a virtue of poverty.
> He goes his way
> Without relying on others

And does not pride himself
On walking alone.
While he does not follow the crowd
He won't complain of those who do.
Rank and reward
Make no appeal to him;
Disgrace and shame
Do not deter him.
He is not always looking
For right and wrong
Always deciding "yes" or "no."
The ancient said, therefore:

"The man of Tao
remains unknown
perfect virtue
produces nothing
'No-self'
is 'True-Self.'
And the greatest man
Is Nobody."[5]

Good is good when it has become good for nothing. If this good is for something, then that something has already negated its goodness, neutralizing it. Is it still good? The "good for something" has finally become good for nothing. That which is truly good must be good for nothing. When there is nothing to be gained, good remains. That is why Chuang Tzu's ethicist is the person who is good for nothing, the person whose left hand is unaware of the activity of the right hand. A truly kind person is the person who does not know that he or she is kind. A generous person does not understand generosity. A bold person does not know that she acts boldly. A giving person gives into nothing because to give for something becomes commercializing. A philanthropist does not know the meaning of philanthropy so that "good" remains in the face of nothing. To be good is to be good for nothing. To be good for something is not being good; it's something else.

Nothing in Good and Evil

Good and Evil

We need to take this a step further. The world of an ethicist, technically speaking, is a world of right and wrong, good and evil. It is the world where one analyzes, discriminates, and makes decisions. But Chuang Tzu's ethicist does not discriminate between right and wrong, good and evil. This person agrees with Merton that "as soon as man becomes aware of doing good and avoiding evil, he is no longer perfectly good."[6] This is because one realizes that what is now good may, in time, be bad. What is right may be wrong depending on location. A good Muslim may be a bad Protestant. A good Buddhist may be a bad Muslim. A good Hindu may be a bad Buddhist. To lie or not to lie depends on where one lives. To give or not to give may depend on the stage of one's growth. This is the second nothing in moral action that Chuang Tze invites us to ponder. The second nothing of moral duty is to clear all societal norms so that one may see more clearly. What can one see by so doing?

Discrimination and Disunity

Theologian Dietrich Bonhoeffer eloquently states in the first paragraph of his book *Ethics,* "The knowledge of good and evil seems to be the aim of all ethical reflection. The first task of Christian ethics is to invalidate this knowledge."[7] On the same page he provides an argument:

> Already in the possibility of the knowledge of good and evil Christian ethics discerns a falling away from the origin. Man at his origin knows only one thing: God. It is only in the unity of his knowledge of God that he knows of other men, of things, and of himself. He knows all things only in God, and God in all things. The knowledge of good and evil shows that he is no longer at one with this origin.[8]

Thinking in terms of good and bad presupposes that we cannot remain where we are. The "is" is not good enough. We find ourselves at a place where we are not supposed to be. So, in an attempt to be where we think we ought to be, we think in terms of good and evil, right and wrong. It is a struggle for a sense of worthiness. A person who constantly struggles with a conflicting sense of good and evil is a person who is trapped within himself or herself, a conflicted person, a person who is neither at ease nor at peace. In describing the Pharisees, Bonhoeffer writes:

> Every moment of life becomes a situation of conflict in which he has to choose between good and

> evil. For the sake of avoiding any lapse his entire thought is strenuously devoted night and day to the anticipation of the whole immense range of possible conflicts, to the reaching of a decision in these conflicts, and to the determination of his own choice. There are innumerable factors to be observed, guarded against and distinguished. The finer the distinctions, the surer will be the correct decision. This observation extends to the whole of life in all its manifold aspects.[9]

This is the struggle of a person who attempts to be in unity with God. The paradox is that the struggle itself implies the disunion. In being apart, one tries to be united. A person in union does not need to try. When a rich young ruler asked Jesus how to be saved, he knew that the answer would be "to love God with all your heart and to love your neighbor as yourself." But who is my neighbor? Jesus told the story of a good Samaritan. While the scholar and the priest struggled with ceremonial laws and rituals, the Samaritan was free from all these conflicts. The Samaritan did not have to think "right and wrong." He saw the man in need, assisted, and did not care about any recognition. He only wanted to pay the bills. He was not trying to avoid making mistakes. He was not plagued by conflicting decisions. He was not trying to be anything.

This constant struggle with right and wrong only hurts the soul. Take food as an example. When it is wrong to eat, one becomes obsessed with it. This process of self-judging takes pleasure away from savoring the flavor. The eating continues. Speaking of the impact this type of discrimination has on individuals with eating disorders, Janet Carr and Marian Eberly write: "Labeling food as 'good' and 'bad' influences food intake. . . . Extreme elimination of foods labeled 'bad' is a hallmark of anorexia, and clearly leads to serious mal-nourishment."[10] Another danger, according to Carr and Eberly, is that labeling leads to inappropriate moral judgment. "When 'bad' food is consumed, people may judge themselves 'bad' based on their food intake. . . . When eating is equated with morality, guilt may mount with each bite of a 'bad' food."[11]

Awareness

Without thinking about "right and wrong," how does one go about living? There is a tendency to think that Chuang Tzu does not care about morality.[12] Yet Chuang Tzu seems to suggest a prescription on how one is to live. Chuang Tzu's butterfly is a metaphor for transformation, a transformation that takes place naturally. Often this transformation is inhibited by artificial imposition of ideas on nature. If there is to be a "wrong" in Chuang Tzu, it is that violence against nature. The flow of life takes place in the alignment of self with what is, by listening to life, paying attention to, and observing things. In the afterword to *A Night Without Armor,* Jewel Kelcher has succinctly captured the reality of our day-to-day lives when she writes,

> Poetry is honest. It is not celebrity selling itself with perfect-image marketing: perfectly slim, perfectly happy, perfectly talented. As a child watching television and reading magazines, I felt separate from what seemed to be a race of people

> who were born extraordinary, with no problems, no hate, no abuse, no hurt. Reading Neruda and Bukowski showed me humans who were good, but also struggling. I could learn from their honesty about their vanity, envy, and self-pity, as well as their hopes for goodness.[13]

Perhaps when we walk through life, observing it, we will become aware of its poetry and recognize as Jewel did.

> As a child I walked
> with noisy fingers
> along the hemline
> of so many meadows
> back home
>
> Green fabric
> stretched out
> shy earth
> shock of sky
>
> I'd sit on logs like pulpits
> listen to the sermon
> of sparrows
> and find god in Simplicity,
> there amongst the dandelion
> and thorn[14]

When one becomes more aware without struggles, without any judgment, one sees more clearly. When viewed as such, we can probably say it is not as if there is no right and wrong in Chuang Tzu's writings. In chapter two of the Inner Chapters he suggests that if right were really right, it should be so clear that there is no need to argue about it. Perhaps there is a right and a wrong, but it is about the right to be wrong and the right to belong. It is about making decision without inner conflicts. It is about doing that no longer adds or subtracts anything from a sense of who one is. And when one just is, one moves with ease, easily wondering around flittering, fluttering like a butterfly.

Absolutely Nothing

The final nothing is a reflection on the very ground of ethics itself. As stated earlier, the teaching of Chuang Tzu is about aligning oneself with nature, with what is. The interesting thing is that "what is" is constantly changing. It is not constant, stable, static, or fixed. It moves and flows. There is no fixed-absolute, the object of Descartes' quest for the *cogito*. What is absolute is change itself. There is no reality behind the phenomena, and we are a part of this reality, transforming and being transformed by it.[15] Reality is not something we need to discover through philosophical methodologies. It is not something out there. We are in the midst of it. We are a part of it. We change it. It changes us. And as long as humanity exists on this planet, through thoughts, deeds, and words, it can never remain the same. Here one comes to realize that one becomes that very ground for truth validation in the midst of the permeating Absolute that one knows not. And yet it is the nothingness of this Absolute that everything breathes and moves and has its being.

Roger Ames's understanding of the concept of knowing in classical Chinese tradition is helpful here. "Knowing is always practical, contingent, and moral: it is a 'doing' rather than a state of mind. Further, 'Knowing' is meliorative—it makes a situation better. 'Knowing' is thus more pragmatic than theoretical."[16] Hence according to Chuang Tzu, there is no distinction between thinking and doing. Thinking is praxis. Its aim is practical. It does not seek to discover truth that stands behind the phenomena. The connectedness between thinking and doing seems to suggest that interacting with our reality means changing it and being changed by it.

Ethics and Playfulness: Theological Approach

What is intriguing about Chuang Tzu's approach is his ability to be playful. Perhaps Chuang Tzu can afford to be playful because even though the Tao is unknown, it is there, moving, changing, and guiding. It is organic and while the sage sits, the sun shines, rain falls, and crops grow. What is needed is to be empty and let emptiness lead to a greater awareness of nature, and in this awareness, we may align ourselves. On "Making All Things Equal," Chuang Tzu uses the earth metaphor to illustrate the role of nature, or what he calls the "piping of heaven." The hallows of the earth can produce great music when "the Great Clod belches out breath and its name is wind."[17] Hence emptiness is meaningful only in relation to the piping of heaven. Reality is not just abandoned humanity trying to make something out of the fact that we are here. Reality is the intimate interchange between us and the world. "Heavenly piping," writes Kuang-ming Wu, "is the spring power (*chi*) and seed-power (*chung*) of all pipings."[18] In this juncture, the choice we have to make is not between right and wrong. Arguing for the moral imperative of Chuang Tzu, Eske Møllgaard states:

> For Zhuangzi, the fundamental choice is, paradoxically, the "choice" of our own fate and nature, what we are, or, as it is also named in the Zhuangzi, "the reality of our nature and destiny" (*xingming zhiquing*). Without this choice, moral action, the choice between right and wrong, will decline into moralism and technicalities . . . from which our judgments issue "like arrows from the cross-bow trigger," that is to say, our moral judgment becomes deadly to others.[19]

Nuan and the Ethics of Chuang Tzu

We need once again to return to Nuan and ask what Chuang Tzu might have prescribed in her situation. What should be done to a father who betrays his daughter? Betrayal is wrong. It is an act of violence against another soul. But it is a symptom of an idea. Buffalos are no longer sufficient and dress codes alter norms. It is a symptom of an idea that pathologizes webbed toes and chopped feet. It is a symptom of an idea that perpetuates a hierarchy of wants. An idea has made buffalos undesirable. An idea has made a thatch roof unlivable. Symptoms have to be dealt with, but symptoms are symptoms. Corruptions, betrayal, abuse, and deceitfulness are symptoms of a self trapped in its own creation of the hierarchy of desire and wants. Discrimination emerges from norms, a deviation from standards.

Chuang Tzu invites us to the forest. Because that is what one needs to see. Thus Taoist political theory sees a society of people living in harmony with one another and with nature, free from the oppressive state of interference and economic oppression, "an egalitarian, non-aggressive, co-operative society."[20] It sees a society ruled by a noninterfering government where leaders live by example, promoting simplicity without discrimination.

However, Taoism is also known to have inspired the Boxer Rebellion and other secret societies "encouraging radical ideas and anti-imperial insurgency."[21] As pointed out by Isabelle Robinet, these Taoist-inspired periodic rebellions were engaged in view of the restoration of peace and order that were compromised by a failing dynasty.[22] On this political engagement, J. J. Clarke writes:

> It would certainly be false to maintain that Daoists have never been involved in warfare, or even that they were pacifists in principle, but it is important to note that their concern with military and pugilistic methods was based on a recognition of the inevitability of violence rather than its desirability, and was associated with the attempt to formulate means of dealing with conflict in the least destructive of ways and on the refinement of defensive techniques which minimize the use of force.[23]

The symptoms will have to be dealt with, but it is always in view of the bigger picture. Again one is reminded of P'eng and the ninety thousand *li*'s journey. It is not that P'eng has gone off to another universe; P'eng still lives among us, but nothing looks the same anymore. One is reminded of postenlightenment monks who continue to scrub floors and carry water even though everything has changed for them.

Monkeying Around

It would be wrong to assume that Chuang Tzu is all about deviation from norms; that all he asks us to do is to totally disregard social etiquettes, codes of conducts, or traffic rules. Conventions such as which fork to use first when seated at a formal dining event may not be things Chuang Tzu opposes. As a matter of fact, how to behave at a concert hall may even be of interest to him. What has to be remembered, however, is that all these things have to be carried out with the awareness that they in no way have the power to define who we are. We are not more or less sophisticated because of which fork we use for soup or dessert (that is why a chopstick is a clever solution!). To Chuang Tzu, we are just monkeying around, and it can be fun. We are not less or more scholarly based on the criteria set by some prestigious higher institutions. We are not more or less religious, polite, clever, or moral. Since we live in a society in which people need to define others, it is probably unwise to step on toes unnecessarily. So we go on monkeying around, realizing that we are playing games that in no way define who we are. Chuang Tzu would have told us to be good sports, play the game, have fun, and forget about winning or losing.

Summary

In this chapter I propose that to be a good ethicist, if there is such a thing, is to be good for nothing. The first nothing is the nothing in return. To do good for something only neutralizes itself and therefore negates its goodness. A person who does good, according to Chuang Tzu, does not even recognize that he or she is doing something good. The second nothing involves clearing away the categories of right and wrong, good and evil. This is significant for two reasons. Created categories are often relative and pertain mostly to time and place. They are not universal. Depending on the time and place, good can be bad, and bad can be good. Commenting on Chuang Tzu's "Lady Beautiful," Kuang-ming Wu writes:

> Chuang Tzu has produced three points. Firstly things are as they are, each in its own way responding to others. Secondly, things are so interdependent that universally valid judgement is impossible. When we say or argue one thing about a particular case, we must at the same time say or argue something else about it. Thirdly, the validity of judgement depends on the perspective from which it is made. And the perspective depends on the subject, which is not unchanging.[24]

We create categories as a means of feeling good about ourselves, which implies that we do not like what we have in the first place. This in no way suggests total relativity. If this were so, Chuang Tzu would not discuss transformation. What is important is for each individual to recognize that we must each make our path. Numerous criteria and standards only inflict pain in our lives and have been created because of our dissatisfaction with what is. Hence we need to free ourselves from these categories so we can engage in what really matters for each of us. This is true nonaction. Møllgaard writes: "For nonaction is not the absence of actions; it is, rather, the highest and most ethical form of action."[25] The final nothing is the nothing that rests on the basis of our action. Because reality is changing and because we are a part of this reality, we play an important role in changing reality itself. What we do determines reality itself. However, Chuang Tzu would have added that this praxis does not have to be taken with such seriousness. We can be at ease because nature is organic. In emptiness, the piping of heaven is able to produce a mesmerizing symphony.

Conclusion
Be Ordinary

無為

In Wey there was an ugly man named Ai Tai-T'o. Women who had seen him wanted to be with no one else. He advocated nothing but following others. He did not occupy a high position nor acquired a salary to feed others. He was uglier than anyone under heaven. He followed along and took no lead. Yet he was constantly surrounded by people.

—CHUANG TZU

PERHAPS A GLIMPSE of freedom is reflected in an image of a person who finds satisfaction in just being ordinary. It is freeing to be ordinary. When one has to strive to be something more than what one truly is, one moves into the area of the "conditional." In this circle, life is determined by social structures. In the conditional, one betrays one's very self. Hence to move toward the unconditional may just be the journey toward the ordinary. To just "be" in the ordinary sense of the word is liberating. It is serene. It frees us to become the very being from which we were called by God. It releases us from pretentious public obligation. It offers a space for us to breathe deeply, and it invites our souls to the realm of rhythm and poetry. In the unconditional, one moves and flows, reshuffling and reconfiguring. In the transformation of self, one just becomes. "The simple and the mundane," writes Kuang-ming Wu, "is now a spectacular mirror of the deep darkness, the lake of heaven, the heavenly reservoir of existence."[1]

It will be a mistake to even entertain the thought that Chuang Tzu is promoting some form of anti-institutional behaviors or the "be-yourself" pop-psychology. His view of life permeates beneath the thick surface of the different names we give to the sociological and cultural realities. He invites us to transcend all the names that have been named and recognize our ability to turn illusion into what we think is real. His invitation is not a reaction toward institutionalized societal norms and standards but an engagement in the things that really matter by peeling off layers of illusion so we may be capable of remaining fully in the present.

I remember vividly as a teenager sitting on a bus one afternoon. Two old Chinese ladies got on, one at the front and the other, the back. They wore funny clothes. They were clumsy but cheery, carrying funny stuff with them. They talked loudly, exchanging information about their husbands so that all forty-five of the passengers on the bus could hear. And I thought then, "How embarrassing!" But now I wish I could be like these two, these old self-differentiated ladies. They were free and liberated. They had no need to fit in. They had no need to strive. They were just two old Chinese ladies happily traveling on the bus, having a great conversation and sharing it with the bus's passengers.

Perhaps this is what Chuang Tzu means when he suggests that one should do nothing. Transformation takes place not in doing something but in doing nothing. Why do something when one can do nothing? But Chuang Tzu goes deeper. One can't even aim at transforming because by so doing one achieves only its negation. This is true with happiness. One can't aim for happiness. Happiness happens by itself and when it happens, one is happy. "Do nothing," says Chuang Tzu. One's effort cannot add or subtract from the quality of the person that one is. "Doing" to be somebody is subtracting the self from oneself because one is further removed from the person that one is. Do nothing to try to modify, change, transform, or fix yourself. Do everything else from the self that needs no fixing. Don't try to achieve a self. It already is. Be still and let it speak to you because the transformation of the self is not an ideal to achieve. When it happens, it happens. The path is unknown. The way is not named. Do nothing, and one may or may not get there because there is no "there" to get to. When one is, one just is. An enlightened monk continues carrying buckets of water and mopping the floor as diligently as before. But nothing is ever the same. Everything has changed. "Do nothing," says Chuang Tzu. Be a nobody and leap ninety thousand *li*.

In chapter six of the inner chapters Chuang Tzu reflects on what it means to be a real person:

> What is a true man? The true man of old did not oppose the minority, did not strive for heroic

> accomplishments, and did not scheme over affairs. Such being the case, he did not regret it when he made a mistake nor feel smug when he was right. Such being the case, he could climb high without trembling, enter water without getting soaked, and enter fire without feeling hot. Only one whose knowledge can ascend the heights of the Way can be like this.[2]

In our quest for spirituality, the way is unknown, the path is unnamed. Transformation takes place not by transforming. We live in a noisy society. There are many voices that keep reminding us of what we ought to be, of various standards and multiple criteria. These noises make us want to move in various directions, complying to their callings. In the midst of these seductive invitations remains a lost soul. Silence, on the other hand, is how we come to really hear the essence of who we are. Not by judging nor analyzing but just listening. The soul finds its destiny. Be ordinary. Flow in the stream of life, and you may be awakened to find yourself ninety thousand *li* from the beginning of your spiritual journey. Be ordinary, and you may just get there without going anywhere. The Way is here. The Way is there. The Way is everywhere. We have all gone too far too long in search of life. Chuang Tzu invites us to just stay, stay in the ordinariness of life. Jasmin Lee Cori provides a possible description of such a person:

> Running through the village
> embracing everyone she meets,

she laughs in ecstasy.
People call her *mad*.

"New eyes!" she cries.
"I have been given new eyes!"
And it is true.
For the scales which had previously blinded her
are gone now, erased
revealing such utter glory
that her mind took flight,
leaving only a rapturous heart
in an old, weathered body
racing through the streets
on fire with love.[3]

Ordinariness is not a project to be pursued. It is the quality of the soul. Stay. Just stay. Stay in the peak of happiness, in the depth of sorrow, in the moment of excitement, in the darkness of pain. Stay. And when one stays long enough to hear the voice of silence that speaks so utterly clear, one may find that the Way is already here.

Appendix A
Chuang Tzu: Historical Background

The people known as the Shang or Yin lived along the Yellow River in north central China around 1000 BCE. Little is known of their origin except that their civilization was relatively old and rich. They were conquered by the Chou, a neighboring group of people that ultimately became the Chou Dynasty, the longest dynasty in Chinese history. The Chou Dynasty lasted for a period of a little over four centuries. Its authority was undermined during the Spring and Autumn Period (771–476 BCE). Division emerged. The deterioration of the Chou Dynasty continued during the Warring States Period (475–221 BCE), resulting in pain, suffering, injustice, bloodshed, and chaos. The world of religion was deeply affected as well. Reverence and respect for divinity was replaced by manipulation through ritual practices. The gods must be pleased to avoid punishment. Hence humoring the heavenly host with sacrifices, rites, and prayers kept away human misery—at least, so they hoped. But such practices only added to the deterioration of the Chou Dynasty. Order, morality, and peace must be restored to the people. For this reason, the search for such a method, for the Way, preoccupied the generation. They wanted a way out of this chaos. But which way is the right way? Is there the Way? Some suggested more rules while others, more love. Some pleaded for more respect while others, greater authority. They were searching for the Way. But many ways were proposed. Out of this chaos came one of the most exciting intellectual and philosophical eras in Chinese history. The fame of the Chou Dynasty rests chiefly on the development of extensive literature and philosophical thinking that started sometime around the sixth century BCE from individuals such as Confucius, Mencius, Lao Tzu, and Chuang Tzu.

Confucius

It was late during this period that the "knight" arose as an intellectual group that sought new political theories. Confucius was one of such knights. He was born in 551 BCE in the state of Lu in modern Shantung. His family name was K'ung. As a young man, he served in minor posts in Lu. At the age of fifty-one, he became a magistrate and the minister of justice in the same year. Confucius, sensing his destiny, gave himself the task of being a social reformer. Not a philosopher in a technical sense, his philosophy nevertheless exerted a great influence on Chinese civilization.[1] The social context of Confucius' era was one of political disunity that undermined religions, moral codes, and political institutions of the declining Chou Dynasty. Confucius was determined to restore morality and order to the society, advocating punctiliousness in the performance of rites and sacrifices. These rites, unlike their prior conceptions, had no magic in themselves. They have to be pleasing to the gods. To Confucius, moral character was the root of civilization, and he believed that outward behaviors reflected the qualities of the inner lives.[2]

Mo Ti

Late in the fifth century, a man by the name of Mo Ti (also known as Mo Tzu), a rival of Confucius, proposed a principle of universal love as the new foundation for the reformation of the crumbling Chinese society.[3] This universal love is spelled out in our love for God. Therefore the question we need to consider is, "What does God want and what does God hate?" God wants humanity to love and to live for one another. We are called to do the will of God and avoid what God hates. "Those who love others will be loved by others. Those who benefit others will be benefited by others."[4] It is not punctiliousness and moral uprightness that can restore order. Love, Mo Ti claimed, was that Way.

Shang Yang

Shang Yang, the successor of Mo Ti, was, like Mo Ti, a utilitarian. But, unlike Mo Ti, he was very zealous and single-minded. His views are preserved in the *Book of Lord Shang*. Shang Yang was known as China's Machiavelli-in-action. He advocated detailed laws and enforced heavy punishment. His school became known as *Fa Chia,* or the Legalists.[5] The problem with our society, Shang Yang believed, is not because there isn't enough love, punctiliousness, or respect. We all know what we should do. The problem is, we do not have the courage to enforce, to implement. Discipline is what we lack. The Way is the courage to enforce discipline and punishment.

Yang Chu

There is no systematic collection of Yang Chu's ideas, and hence it has to be deduced from scattered references. It is speculated that he lived between the time of Mo Ti (479–381 BCE) and Mencius[6] (371–289 BCE).[7] Yang Chu's teachings advocate the practice of the preservation of life. Some of the phrases that reflect Yang Chu's teaching appear, at first look, hedonistic. In describing Yang Chu's philosophy, Mencius says: "The principle of Yang Chu is: 'Each one for himself.' Though he might have profited the whole world by plucking out a single hair, he would not have done it."[8] The hedonistic tone of "not plucking out a single hair to save the world" is better understood in the light of Yang Chu's assumptions, which are "each one for himself" and "despising things and valuing life." In the Taoist text Lieh-tzu,[9] Yang Chu is reported to have said:

> The men of antiquity, if by injuring a single hair they could have profited the world, would not have done it. Had the world been offered to them as their exclusive possession, they would not have taken it. If everybody would refuse to pluck out even a single hair, and everybody would refuse to take the world as a gain, then the world would be in perfect order.[10]

And so the history of ideas moved from one extreme to the other, counterbalancing one another as an attempt to arrive at the Way. But counterbalancing things is still within the realm of the conditional. The Way is beyond. And to this beyond came the writings of Lao Tzu and Chuang Tzu.

What happened after these movements was described by translator Angus Graham.

> As the rival schools multiplied, debate became progressively more rational, until late in the fourth century BC sophists appeared who studied logical puzzles for their own sake. Chuang-tzu was a younger acquaintance, perhaps at some time a disciple, of the greatest of the sophists, Hui Shih. But he turned away from him, towards the cult of intuitiveness and spontaneity in both political and private action which was to become characteristic of Taoism.[11]

Appendix B
The Psychology of Nondoing

無為

A man is supple and weak when living, but hard and stiff when dead. Grass and trees are pliant and fragile when living, but dried and shrivelled when dead. Thus the hard and the strong are the comrades of death; the supple and the weak are the comrades of life. Therefore a weapon that is strong will not vanquish; a tree that is strong will suffer the axe. The strong and big takes the lower position, the supple and weak takes the higher position.

—Lao Tzu

Introduction

Water flows. There is a certain beauty in this image. I have spent a major part of my life trying to conquer and control life, and yet there is something enticing and mystical about its "flow." Alan Watts' description of Taoists that states, "They have no design to subjugate or alter the universe by force or will-power, for their art is entirely to go along with the flow of things in an intelligent way"[1] makes me want to find out more about the possible relation between the "flow" and our psyche.

"To flow" suggests the ability to adapt shape and form in order to follow the course of gravity. It is the ability to move along the line of least resistance. From a philosophical point of view, the world and reality is not about knowing and grasping through the rational process. Attempts at placing the world into a consistent logical conclusion uproot life from its natural form; it resists the natural flow of life.[2]

Flow

If reality is bigger than what the mind can grasp, or as Stanley Cavell has stated, "There is something in the self that logically cannot be brought to knowledge,"[3] then our task is not trying to fit things into certain preconceived forms but to observe life as it comes. Commenting on the writings of Chuang Tzu, Kuang-ming Wu writes:

> His rationality is a power that deepens the reader's sentiments and heightens his sensitivity to life. His is a reason exclusive of traditional reason, but inclusive of the reason of the heart. . . . If there is reason in the heart that reason knows not, the heart-reason that includes both is anything but irrational. Such reason has a certain inevitability and necessity that is intelligible to a reasonable person, a man of the world.[4]

Hence if one is to understand life, one needs to observe

the rhythm and flow of life. "To observe" suggests that life does speak to us, and we need to listen to what it has to say. Chinese doctors are known for saying, "Your heart is trying to tell you something. Listen to your heart."

Letting Go/Flowing

The language of "letting go" plays a significant role in human psychological process as inherent in the prayer of Reinhold Neibuhr, "God, give us grace to accept with serenity the things that cannot be changed, courage to change the things that should be changed, and the wisdom to distinguish the one from the other."[5] At a deeper level, "letting go" is about letting go of any attempt at defining "being" for ourselves. It is instead about allowing "being" to reveal itself to us. It is about sitting down and observing the phenomenon of "being" as it unfolds itself. To observe "being" is to allow "being" to reveal itself. "Being" reveals itself when we stop trying to force "being" into a certain mode of being but allow the self to experience that which is, and through this "isness," come to an understanding of the self.

If emotional trauma and pain are caused by conflict that emerges from "being" resisting being defined through rational process or placed into a logical system, then finding "being" by allowing this "being" to speak to us and flowing along can potentially bring about the relief of psychological trauma and emotional pain in one's life. When we are trying to "be" what we are not, believing that who we are not is what we really are, then life and our internal psychic process turn against us. This blocks the natural flow of our psyche and our life. We become enemies to ourselves. The blocking of the natural flow is exhibited in various forms. In *Better Than Blessed,* Donald L. Anderson writes:

> Only very recently have we begun to realize that to deny grief is to deny a natural human function and that such denial sometimes produces dire consequences. . . . Grief, like any genuine emotion, is accompanied by certain physical changes and the release of a form of psychic energy. If that energy is not expended in the normal process of grieving, it becomes destructive within the person.[6]

The above example is just one out of many possible damages we can do to our psyche if we resist the natural flow of life. In describing the Taoist sage, Lao Tzu writes: "He doesn't think about his actions; they flow from the core of his being."[7] In this same concept Chaung Tzu states:

> I have heard of letting the world be, and exercising forbearance; I have not heard of governing the world. Letting be is from the fear that men, (when interfrered with), will carry their nature beyond its normal condition; exercising forbearance is from the fear that men, (when not so dealt with), will alter the characteristics of their nature. When all men do not carry their nature beyond its normal condition, nor later its characteristics, the good government of the world is secured.[8]

Three Concepts

There are basically three concepts[9] that I find pertinent to the human psyche: *Li, yin* and *yang,* and *wu wei. Li* may be translated as that which makes it what it ought to be. *Yin* and *yang* refers to the paradox of life. It implies that one needs to seek to strive for balance in life. *Wei wu wei* means "to do without doing or to act without acting." These three concepts can be conceptualized in Taoist understanding of nature. Nature has its own course and flow. In order to find and fulfill the natural flow of nature, one needs to learn to "sit around and do nothing" and let nature takes its course; one needs to learn to flow with nature. In describing this "flow," Alan Watts writes: "Thus the Tao is the course, the flow, the drift, or the process of nature, and I call it the Watercourse Way because both Lao-tzu and Chuang Tzu use the flow of water as its principal metaphor."[10]

> Chao-Chou asked, "What is the Tao?"
>
> The master (Nan-chuan) replied, "Your ordinary consciousness is the Tao."
>
> "How can one return into accord with it?"
>
> "By intending to accord you immediately deviate."
>
> "But without intention, how can one know the Tao?"
>
> "The Tao," said the master, "belongs neither to knowing nor to not knowing. Knowing is false understanding; not knowing is blind ignorance.

> If you really understand the Tao beyond doubt, it's like the empty sky. Why drag in right and wrong?"[11]

Li

Li makes what is is. It regulates itself. Nature cannot be preconceived conceptually. Nature can be learned but not taught. Nature is broader than what words can describe. Nature "is." History is filled with stories of people seeking to grasp and define nature. In seeking to define nature, we limit "nature" to that which we can conceive, that which can be categorized in human terms. In seeking to grasp "nature," we limit "nature" to our thought forms derived from our vocabulary. Having arrived at what "nature" is, we stipulate the "ought" and dictate how beings should behave. We tell "us" what we ought to be, what we ought to feel. We tell ourselves that if we were other than what we have conceived ourselves to be, then perhaps we are not in line with "nature." We tell ourselves that if we feel other than that which we have defined, perhaps we are not feeling right. We seek to define "nature" and allow this definition to dictate our mode of being. In his introduction to *The Texts of Taoism,* D. T. Suzuki writes:

> Your very attempt to explain betrays the fact that you do not know anything about them. Do Heaven and Earth ever talk about the course they follow day and night? Do the sun and the moon argue about their shining over us? The Heavenly Tao just pursues its natural course and does not discourse about it. So let the human way be,

> too. We must just leave the Great Tao alone and keep our steps with it. It is all-embracing, all sufficient: great is great and has no desire to become other than itself; small is small and has no hankering for anything else.[12]

Chuang Tzu teaches that "nature" transcends thought forms, logic, and language. "Nature" cannot be captured. "Nature" just is. We cannot predefine our "ought" conceptually. We cannot arrive at the understanding of who we are and what we should do through cognitive reflection. Life cannot be predefined. Life has to be observed.

From psychological perspectives, we have observed that resistance damages one's emotional well-being. Take, for example, grief. In resisting the process of grief that takes its natural course, one can turn normal grief to pathological grief. "Grief that is inhibited or denied expression is potentially pathogenic because the bereaved person avoids dealing with the reality of the loss."[13] When we disallow "nature" to take its course, we block its flow. When that happens, "nature" turns against us. There is only one way for "nature" to take its course, and that course is the "natural course." When it does not happen, it becomes unnatural.

One way of resisting the flow of being is seen in our wanting to rush into solving life's problems. We are not comfortable with problems in life. We are not able to accept that problems are a part of the process of life. In our discomfort, we rush in trying to solve the existing problems. Defense mechanisms are one way we express our discomfort with problems and pain. In our inability to stay with the pain within our lives, we defend ourselves, we protect ourselves from getting hurt. In this defense, the "brain deceives itself daily from the pain of seeing the truth."[14] The self deceives itself because defense mechanisms are "the ways people react to frustration and conflict by deceiving themselves about their real desires and goals in an effort to maintain their self-esteem and avoid anxiety."[15] In experiencing pain, the self seeks a way out of this discomfort. To achieve this, we map out the causes of our pain. Reality has been dissected and named. Causal relation has been figured. Once again, in solving problems, we fall back on our categorical thinking that we have imposed on "being."

Commenting on Heidegger's approach to being, Hans-Georg Gadamer writes, "The real question is not in what way being can be understood but in what way understanding *is* being."[16] In line with this concept, T. L. Orcutt and J. R. Prell suggest that perhaps the best way to deal with conflict is to accept its actuality. Accept that this actuality includes anxiety, pain, fear, and death.[17]

Problems we are facing seem to be the result of our resistance to nature, to the flow of nature. We have not learned to trust nature. We try to conquer it. We try to get over it. We try to overcome it. Taoism teaches that we need to learn to trust nature. We trust nature when we learn to "let ourselves be." In learning how to "let ourselves be," we also learn how to let things be, suggests Chuang Tzu.[18] *Li* makes what is is. In the chapter on "Welcoming" in *Grace Unfolding*, Greg Johanson and Ron Kurtz write:

> The sage or master works without judgment. She is a welcoming presence who can allow for and

> embrace all being and nonbeing. Her response to us if we said, "I can't think now" would probably not be, "Yes, you can think. Come on now. Think!" but, "listen to that part of you that can't think. Perhaps it will tell you more about itself." The sage simply attends to and accommodates what is, especially those things which arise spontaneously in our experience. This attitude of acceptance, inclusion, and trust in what is, is not a technique so much as a wordless principle. . . . We are simply empowered by what is, and can move on in a way that does not depend on the therapist's cleverness or insight.[19]

Similarly, Alan Watts suggests that "the art of life is more like navigation than warfare, for what is important is to understand the winds, the tides, the currents, the seasons, and the principles of growth and decay, so that one's actions may use them and not fight them."[20]

Yin *and* Yang

> Bowed down then preserved;
> Bent then straight;
> Hollow then full;
> Worn then new;
> A little then benefited;
> A lot then perplexed.
> Therefore the sage embraces the One and is
> a model for the empire.[21]

"The heavy is the root of the light; the still is the lord of the restless," said Lao Tzu in chapter 27 of *Tao Te Ching*. Taoism teaches that if one is to learn to observe life and reality phenomenologically, one will discern the paradoxical nature of life and reality. Life is paradoxical and therefore it eludes any human attempt to capture it in any logical definable term. Life is cyclical and not linear. Life is both/and and not either/or. Opposites do not exclude each other. Opposites unite.

The practical application to human relationship from an existentialistic viewpoint is expressed by Paul Tillich, who suggests that "in every polarity each pole is limited as well as sustained by the other one."[22] Self is always seeking its own integration. The integration of this self includes both poles. This self is in constant threat of losing one pole or the other and is constantly in need to maintain the tension between finite individualization and finite participation. The pursuit of finite individualization ends in loneliness and alienation from the community. On the other hand, collective participation leads to the loss of individuality and subjectivity. In describing human's anxiety in the face of the possible loss of integration, Tillich writes, "He oscillates anxiously between individualization and participation, aware of the fact that he ceases to be if one of the poles is lost, for the loss of either pole means the loss of both."[23]

Conflict is perceptual. Chuang Tzu teaches that "that the 'that' and the 'this' cease to be opposites is the very essence of Tao. Only this essence, an axis as it were, is the center of the circle responding to the endless changes."[24] He advocates the way of seeing that resolve conflicts.

Wu wei

Wu wei can be translated: "To do without doing. To act without acting." Another descriptive analogy for this phrase is "sitting down doing nothing." Lao Tzu writes:

> The way never acts yet nothing is left undone.
> Should lords and princes be able to hold fast
> to it,
> The myrid creatures will be transformed of their
> own accord.
> After they are transformed, should desire raise
> its head,
> I shall press it down with the weight of the
> nameless uncarved block.
> The nameless uncarved block
> Is but freedom from desire,
> And if I cease to desire and remain still,
> The empire will be at peace of its own accord.[25]

Sitting down doing nothing is not to be taken literally. We are invited by Lao Tzu and Chaung Tzu to "sit down and do nothing" because nature is *tzu-jan*. Things happen of themselves, or, as stated in Zenrin Kushu: "(As I) sit quietly, doing nothing, spring comes and grass grows of itself."[26] We sit down because we cannot go against nature. Any attempt that goes against nature alienates. We need to sit and observe nature. The primary task is not to find quick diagnosis. The aim is not to name and fix but to see therapy as an invitation. The aim is to see nature and follow its course because gravity is energy.[27] Hence to "sit down and do nothing" is to place oneself in the flow of nature. In sitting down, we too observe that nature is paradoxical. In life, we miss what we aim for. Life teaches that what we seek to take hold of often eludes us. In the fear of death, we die breathing. In the acceptance of death, we find life. In craving for love, we live in loneliness. When we do not look for love, love finds us. In seeking to be great, we become small. In allowing ourselves to be small, we experience greatness. In serving, we lead. In leading, we are led. In seeking to rid ourselves of sin, we remain captured by sin. In letting go of the fear of sin, sin no longer has the power over us. In light of this paradoxical nature of nature, Lao Tzu advises us to flow, or as Alan Watts paraphrased Lao Tzu, "Superior *wu-wei* does not aim at *wu-wei* and so it truly is *wu-wei*."[28]

In his description of Chuang Tzu's teaching, Kuang-ming Wu writes:

> We must come back to ourselves and be true to ourselves. For self-responsibility is our prime responsibility, and it consists in letting oneself be. Then we will know how to let things be. If we follow our nature, we will naturally let others follow theirs. We neglect this responsibility at our peril and at everyone else's.[29]

Hence *wu wei* is an invitation by life to understand the process of life itself. In the intrapsychic process, *wu wei* asks that we do not rush into diagnosing and fixing life. We are invited rather to stay with the problem and remain comfortable with the problem. In remaining, we are asked to listen with the deep conviction that life heals itself. In viewing healing as a natural system, Edwin Freidman points out that "life moves toward life. In other words, life does not have to be taught how to do it. The second is that the processes of maturation have their own time frame."[30] He further describes this healing process:

> The healer, in other words, does not have to take responsibility for making health happen, but for discovering the universal forces that make life tick, and then lining up the client's thinking and functioning with those life sustaining forces that have continuously evolved since Creation. One may, therefore, have "faith" in natural processes. You can trust them, and having the confidence to rely on them, can free any healer to defocus the symptom and the attending anxiety, and refocus his or her own efforts on becoming a healing presence, that is, one who tries to promote healing rather than to will it.[31]

In listening, we will learn what life has to teach us. In listening, we will learn that being emerges out of nonbeing, or according to Chuang Tzu, "Being is born of non-being that differs from being, whose not-yet-beginning to not-yet, non-being is."[32] Because being emerges out of non-being, any attempt at being that ignores nonbeing will be futile. That being emerges from nonbeing is paradoxical. Living therefore must be achieved through paradox. We learn about life through death. We overcome fear through embracing fear. We find love not in striving for love. We resolve conflict by learning to stay and be comfortable with conflicts. We solve by not solving.

A story has been related of how psychiatrist Murray Bowen treated a lady who wanted to commit suicide. She came into his office asking for a prescription for sleeping pills, adding that she was going to go home and use them to kill herself. Without looking up, Bowen asked, "Well just how many do you think you'll need?" The lady went home, became nauseated and flushed them down the toilet (this method in dealing with suicide is definitely not what I advocate. It is only meant to illustrate the importance of paradox).[33] Paradox is therapeutic, and so it is with the principle of *wu wei*.

> The movement of the Tao
> By contraries proceeds;
> And weakness marks the course
> Of Tao's mighty deeds.[34]

Johanson and Kurtz summarize the meaning of *wu wei* and its relation to human psyche:

> When something is mysterious, it doesn't quite have a name. For instance, we may experience a slight sense of uneasiness in our chest. If we can resist analyzing this to purge it of its uncontrollable namelessness, it may lead us to fuller understanding. Simply befriending the uneasiness—not trying to change it in any way, allowing it to emerge more fully—leads, perhaps, to

our experience saying yes to the words "fear of conflict." These words are not imposed by our minds. They arise from the mysterious region of not-knowing. Since we are attending receptively to the movements of our consciousness, other information naturally gathers around our uneasy fear.[35]

Notes

Introduction

1. J. Krishnamurti, *In the Light of Silence, All Problems Are Dissolved: Excerpts from J. Krishnamurti's Talks and Writings* (Chennai: Krishnamurti Foundation India, 1992), 3.
2. Ibid., 13.
3. Joe Claro, ed., *The Random House Book of Jokes and Anecdotes* (New York: Random House, 1990), 48–49.
4. Lao Tzu, *Tao Te Ching*, trans. Stephen Mitchell (New York: Harper and Row, 1988), 11. Translation copyright © 1988 by Stephen Mitchell. All material from this translation is reprinted with permission of HarperCollins Publishers.
5. Chuang Tzu, *Chuang Tzu: Basic Writings*, trans. Burton Watson (New York: Columbia University Press, 1996), 25. © 1996 by Columbia University Press. All material from this translation is reprinted with permission from the publisher.

Chapter 1: Chuang Tzu

1. Chuang Tzu, *Chuang Tzu: Basic Writings*, trans. Burton Watson (New York: Columbia University Press, 1996), 63.
2. Ibid., 35–36.
3. According to some accounts, Confucius visited Lao Tzu around 518 BCE. It is also believed that Lao Tzu's son served as a general in 273 BCE, but this could not possibly be true. Chinese tradition accepts the former and places Lao Tzu as twenty years Confucius' senior, while

Western scholars tends to date Lao Tzu at the fourth or even third century BCE. Chinese scholars' opinions on the dating are evenly divided. Scholars in mainland China (since 1949) place Lao Tzu in the later date. The legend that Lao Tzu never really existed but was merely a name given to three different accounts is no longer entertained by scholars. Wing-tsit Chan, comp. and trans., *A Source Book in Chinese Philosophy* (Princeton: Princeton University Press, 1963), 138.

4. Allen Watts, *Tao: The Watercourse Way* (New York: Pantheon Books, 1975), xxii.
5. Ibid. *The Inner Chapters* contain many more stories that record the dialogues between Confucius and Lao Tzu (or Old Tan). See the chapter on "The Dialogues of Confucius and Old Tan" in Chuang-tzu, *Chuang-tzu: The Seven Inner Chapters and Other Writings from the Book Chuang-tzu*, trans. A. C. Graham (London: George Allen & Unwin), 126–34.
6. Chan, *Source Book*, 136.
7. H. G. Creel, *What Is Taoism? And Other Studies in Chinese Cultural History* (Chicago: University of Chicago Press, 1970), 46.
8. Chuang-tzu, *Chuang-tzu: The Seven Inner Chapters*, 4–5. As to the location, scholars held various beliefs. But many believe that he came from Meng, which is probably Honan, south of the Yellow River. Again, no one really knows for certain, but if Meng is actually Honan, Chuang Tzu was most likely a native of the state of Sung.
9. Chan, *Source Book*, 178.
10. Ibid., 178–79. It is interesting to note also the philosophical development of neo-Taoism: The Rationalists. Neo-Taoism is a new term used to describe a philosophy that in the third and fourth century CE was called *hsuan hsueh*, or, literally, "dark learning." The term *hsuan* means dark, abstruse, or mysterious, and it occurs in the first chapter of Lao Tzu. Names associated with this term are Hsiang Hsiu and Kuo Hsiang, who both wrote *Commentary on the Chuang-tzu*. Not much is known of Hsiang Hsiu and Kou Hsiang except that, according to *History of the Chin Dynasty*, both of them were natives of the present Honan Province. While Lao Tzu and Chaung Tzu believe Tao to be Wu in that it is not a thing and therefore cannot be named, Hsiang-Kuo takes it a step further and believes that it is literally "nothing." "The Tao is everywhere, but everywhere it is nothing" (*Commentary on the Chuang-tzu*, ch. 6). The same text states, "In existence, what is prior to things? We say that *Yin* and *Yang* are prior to things. But the *Yin* and *Yang* are themselves things; what

then, is prior to the *Yin* and *Yang*? We may say that *Tzu-jan* [nature or naturalness] is prior to things. But *Tzu-jan* is simply the naturalness of things. Or we may say that the *Tao* is prior to things. But the *Tao* is nothing. Since it is nothing, how can it be prior to things? We do not know what is prior to things, yet things are continuously produced. This shows that things are spontaneously what they are; there is no Creator of things." Hsiang-Kuo's *Commentary on Chuang-tzu* speaks of the need to possess the spirit that transcends the distinctions of things and calls people to live according to himself but not according to others. Fung Yu-lan, *A Short History of Chinese Philosophy: A Systematic Account of Chinese Thought from Its Origin to the Present Day*, ed. Derk Bodde (New York: Free Press, 1948), 221.

11. Chuang Tzu, *Chuang Tzu: Basic Writings*, 4.
12. Ibid., 140.
13. Robert E. Allinson, *Chuang-Tzu for Spiritual Transformation* (New York: State of New York University Press, 1989), 23.
14. Ibid., 26.
15. Victor H. Mair, *Wandering on the Way: Early Taoist Tales and Parables of Chuang Tzu* (Honolulu: University of Hawai'i Press, 1994), xiii. All materiaal from this book is reprinted with permission.
16. Ibid.
17. Ibid., xiv.
18. Cited by ibid., xvi.

Chapter 2: The Way

1. Chuang-tzu, *Chuang-tzu: The Seven Inner Chapters and Other Writings from the Book Chuang-tzu*, trans. A. C. Graham (London: George Allen & Unwin), 36–37.
2. Allen Watts, *Tao: The Watercourse Way* (New York: Pantheon Books, 1975), 38. *Tzu-jan* is translated "naturally, of itself," from *tzu*, self, and *jan*, an adverbial suffix (ly). It means that which happens of itself without prompting and hence is spontaneous. Lao Tzu, *Tao Te Ching*, trans. Stephen Mitchell (New York: Harper and Row, 1988), 40.
3. Chuang Tzu, *Chuang Tzu: Basic Writings*, trans. Burton Watson (New York: Columbia University Press, 1996), 72.
4. Raimundo Panikkar, *A Dwelling Place of Wisdom*, trans. Annemarie S. Kidder (Louisville, KY: Westminster/John Knox Press, 1993), 10.
5. Descartes separated object from subject and plunged the whole philosophical movement into searching for an answer to the riddle of the Cartesian dualism. (Richard Bernstein employed the term "Cartesian

Anxiety.") Cartesian Anxiety, besides referring to a quest for objective knowledge that, to Descartes, is the only solid ground for knowing, is also at the same time related to the journey of finite being searching for a power outside that is big enough to contain finitude. Finitude causes anxiety and the way to cope with this anxiety is to find a God outside of the self. It is a quest for some fixed point, some stable rock upon which we can secure our lives against the precariousness of finite beings (Richard Bernstein, *Beyond Objectivism and Relativism: Science, Hermeneutics and Praxis* [Philadelphia: University of Pennsylvania, 1983], 16–18).

6. Thinking in terms of cause and effect, we often think that the lack of rain causes drought, and a drought causes famine, and famine causes death. The Chinese see this whole process as a single unit or as simply four ways of looking at the same event. It is not causality. Watts, *Tao*, 54. In Western medicine, we are taught that bacteria cause illness. The Chinese, however, believe that bacteria are everywhere. They see illness as a result of the weakening of the immune system that keeps a check on the growth of bacteria. When the immune system is weakened, illness occurs. Hence it is not causality but balance. See Daniel Reid, *The Tao of Health, Sex, and Longevity: A Modern Practical Guide to the Ancient Way* (New York: Simon & Schuster, 1989). When discussing the concept of theodicy, we also see rational attempts at constructing theologies that would explain the existence of evil. From a cause-and-effect mentality, we have seen attempts to explain this phenomena by making God less than absolute (process theology), making God an evolving God (John Mcquarrie), or resort to some form of pragmatism (William James). In Chinese thinking, there is no causality but balance, hence the discussion on theodicy is limited to the idea of resisting the Way of nature.
7. Watts, *Tao*, 20.
8. Cited by C. S. Song, *Theology from the Womb of Asia* (New York: Orbis Books, 1986), 12. It is originally from *Modern Chinese Poetry*, which was translated by Harold Acton and Ch'en Shih-Hsiang.
9. Ibid., 13–14.
10. J. P. Dourley, *The Psyche as Sacrament: A Comparative Study of C. G. Jung and Paul Tillich* (Toronto: Inner City Books, 1981), 48.
11. "At the very roots of Chinese thinking and feeling," says Allan Watts, "there lies the principle of polarity." Watts, *Tao*, 19. *Yin* (negative) and *yang* (positive) represent two poles of cosmic energy. The *yin* and *yang* ideograms reflect the sunny and shady sides of a hill. They are associated with the masculine and feminine, the firm and the yield-

ing, the strong and the weak, the light and the dark, the rising and the falling, heaven and earth, and the spicy and the bland. In this system of thinking, negative is just another aspect of positive. The two are parts of the same reality. One cannot exist without the other. There is no understanding of black without white. There is no appreciation of goodness without evil. They both must coexist. It takes both to keep life moving.

12. Cited by Watts, *Tao,* 23.
13. There are many translations for this phrase, and it is because literally this passage says, "*Tao* can be *Tao* not eternal (or regular) *Tao.*" The second word "*Tao*" could also be rendered "be spoken of" or "to speak," but possibly it was not used in this manner in the third century BCE. A more popular translation is, "The *Tao* which can be spoken of is not the eternal *Tao.*" Following are other possible translations: "The *Tao* that can be told of is not the Absolute *Tao*" (Lin Yutang); "The Way that can be told of is not an Unvarying Way" (Arthur Waley); "The *Tao* that is the subject of discussion is not the true *Tao*" (Old); "The Way that may truly be regarded as the Way is other than a permanent way" (Duyvendak); "The Flow that can be discoursed is not the eternal Course" (auct.); "The course that can be discoursed is not the eternal Course" (auct.); "The Force that is forced isn't true Force" (auct.). Arthur F. Wright, ed., *Studies in Chinese Thought* (Chicago: University of Chicago Press, 1953), 38–39.
14. Cited by Watts, *Tao,* 42.
15. Ibid., 55.
16. Cited by ibid., 49.
17. Lao Tzu, *Way of Life: A New Translation of the Tao Te Ching,* trans. Raymond B. Blackney (New York: New American Library, 1955), 100.
18. Ibid., 87.
19. Ibid., 56.
20. Cited by Watts, *Tao,* 38.
21. Cited by ibid., 43.

Chapter 3: Nothing

1. Lao Tzu, *Tao Te Ching,* trans. Stephen Mitchell (New York: Harper and Row, 1988), 11.
2. We strive to be rich, powerful, successful, cool, smart, and righteous, but isn't this precisely the beginning of suffering? We live in a culture that glorifies people who think big and condemns those who think small. We like firm muscles and cute butts. We love style and

glorify youth. We strive for success and are pleased when applauded. And meanwhile we suffer when we are not where we think we ought to be.

3. Carl Jung, *The Portable Jung*, ed. Joseph Campbell (New York: Penguin, 1971), 145–62.
4. Martin Heidegger, *Being and Time* (New York: Harper & Row, 1962), 279–347.
5. This statement reminds me of the logically meaningless *koans* (paradoxical stories) used by Zen masters. A *koan* is not employed to help a person achieve a cause or "attain a limited result, but in order that he may learn to get along definitively without any illusory need to attain anything or to rest in anything." Thomas Merton, *Mystics and Zen Masters* (New York: Noonday Press, 1967), 240.

Chapter 4: Nothing and the Journey of Ninety Thousand Li

1. *Li* in the traditional Chinese unit of measurement for distance and represents approximately half a kilometer.
2. Chuang Tzu, *Chuang Tzu: Basic Writings*, trans. Burton Watson (New York: Columbia University Press, 1996), 46.
3. Ibid., 46–47.
4. Ibid., 25.
5. Ibid., 25–26.
6. Kuang-ming Wu, *The Butterfly as Companion: Meditations on the First Three Chapters of the Chuang Tzu* (New York: State University of New York Press, 1990), 76.
7. Ibid.
8. Ann Belford Ulanov, *Finding Space: Winnicott, God, and Psychic Reality* (Louisville, KY: Westminster John Knox, 2001), 12.
9. Ibid., 15.
10. D. W. Winnicott, *Playing and Reality* (London: Tavistock, 1971), 103.
11. Wu, *Butterfly as Companion*, 73.
12. Ibid., 76.
13. Ibid., 79.
14. Gerald May, *Simply Sane* (New York: Crossroad, 1977), 46.

Chapter 5: Do Nothing

1. Lao Tzu, *Tao Te Ching*, trans. Stephen Mitchell (New York: Harper and Row, 1988), 45.
2. Chuang Tzu, *Wandering on the Way: Early Taoist Tales and Parables*

of Chuang Tzu, trans. Victor Mair (Honolulu: University of Hawai'i Press, 1994), 182–83.

3. Peter Kramer, *Listening to Prozac* (New York: Viking, 1993), 207.
4. James Hillman, *The Soul's Code: In Search of Character and Calling* (New York: Warner Books, 1997), 21.
5. Ibid.
6. Ibid., 22.
7. Chuang Tzu, *Chuang Tzu: Basic Writings,* trans. Burton Watson (New York: Columbia University Press, 1996), 72.
8. Gerald May, *Simply Sane* (New York: Crossroad, 1977), 82.
9. J. Krishnamurti, *In the Light of Silence, All Problems Are Dissolved: Excerpts from J. Krishnamurti's Talks and Writings* (Chennai: Krishnamurti Foundation India, 1992), 7.
10. Ibid., 13.
11. Dietrich Bonhoeffer, *Ethics* (New York: McMillan Publishing, 1955), 17. Bonhoeffer does not suggest total abandonment of moral reflection. However, he believes that it must not be the basis of the pursuit of spirituality. Spirituality must be based on connection and not disconnection.
12. May, *Simply Sane,* 102.
13. Chuang Tzu, *Chuang Tzu: Basic Writings,* 36.
14. Richard Young, *Paths of a Prodigal: Explorations into the Deeper Reaches of Spiritual Living* (New York: Larson Publications, 1997), 129.
15. Krishnamurti, *In the Light of Silence,* 57.
16. Ibid., 31.
17. Disney Enterprises, *Disney's Toy Story* (Burbank, CA: Disney Enterprises, 1996).

Chapter 6: The Nothing of Love and the Love of Nothing

1. Chuang Tzu, *The Way of Chuang Tzu,* trans. Thomas Merton (New York: New Direction, 1965), 53.
2. Thomas Moore, *Soul Mates: Honoring the Mysteries of Love and Relationship* (New York: HarperPerennial, 1994), xii.
3. Ibid., 53.
4. Ibid., 54.
5. Leo Buscaglia, *Living, Loving, and Learning* (New York: Fawcett Columbine, 1982), 89.
6. Ibid., 90.
7. Ann Belford Ulanov, *Finding Space: Winnicott, God, and Psychic Reality* (Louisville, KY: Westminster John Knox, 2001), 109.

8. Ibid., 110.

Chapter 7: Good for Nothing

1. Siroj Sorajjakool, *Child Prostitution in Thailand: Listening to Rahab* (New York: Haworth Press, 2003), 9.
2. Ibid., 10.
3. Eske Møllgaard, "Zhuangzi's Religious Ethics," *American Academy of Religion* 71, no. 2 (2003): 366.
4. Thomas Merton, *Mystics and Zen Masters* (New York: Noonday Press, 1967), 49.
5. Chuang Tzu, *The Way of Chuang Tzu,* trans. Thomas Merton (New York: New Directions, 1965), 91–92.
6. Merton, *Mystics and Zen Masters,* 49.
7. Dietrich Bonhoeffer, *Ethics* (New York: MacMillan, 1955), 17.
8. Ibid.
9. Ibid., 27.
10. Janet K. Carr and Marian C. Eberly, "Nutrition Philosophy," *The Remuda Review: The Christian Journal of Eating Disorders* 2, no. 2 (2003): 2.
11. Ibid.
12. In his chapter on "The Question of Relativism," Allinson discusses five models of looking at Chuang Tzu's "this" and "that." Hard relativism refers to the belief that everything in Chuang Tzu is relativistic. Hence Chuang Tzu is not in any way proposing any position (H. G. Creel, Chad Hansen, Livia Knaul). Soft relativism refers to partial relativism. This view is supported by authors such as Antonio Cua, Angus Graham, and David Wong. According to this position, Chuang Tzu's relativism is de-emphasized when it comes to ethical actions. Neither relativism nor nonrelativism is the next position. It tries to remove Chuang Tzu from this category and ascribes radical perspective to the author (Graham Parkes and the early A. C. Graham). Both relativism and nonrelativism take all statements in Chuang Tzu whether they be relativistic or nonrelativistic, without trying to reduce any to a single position (Russell Goodman). Asymmetrical relativism is the one proposed by Allinson himself. Here relativism applies to the unenlightened mind. But when a person is awakened, this person realizes a value that is of ultimate importance. Robert E. Allinson, *Chuang-Tzu for Spiritual Transformation* (New York: State of New York University Press, 1989), 111–26.
13. Jewel Kelcher, *A Night Without Armor* (New York: HarperEntertainment, 1999), 137. Copyright © 1998 by Jewel Kelcher. Reprinted by permission of HarperCollins Publishers.

14. Ibid., 1.
15. Commenting on this concept, Roger Ames writes: "To say something about the world is to say something about themselves. Their choices, values, and cultural importances are implicit in their interpretations of experience." Roger Ames, "Introduction," in *Yuan Dao: Tracing Dao to Its Source,* trans. D.C. Lao and Rober Ames (New York: Ballantine Books, 1998), 28.
16. Ibid., 26–27.
17. Chuang Tzu, *Chuang Tzu: Basic Writings,* trans. Burton Watson (New York: Columbia University Press, 1996), 31.
18. Kuang-ming Wu, *The Butterfly as Companion: Meditations on the First Three Chapters of the Chuang Tzu* (New York: State University of New York Press, 1990), 187.
19. Møllgaard, "Zhuangzi's Religious Ethics," 365–66.
20. J. J. Clarke, *The Tao of the West: Western Transformations of Taoist Thought* (New York: Routlege, 2000), 109.
21. Ibid., 105.
22. Isabella Robinet, *Taoism: Growth of a Religion, a Translation and Adaptation by Phyllis Brooks of Robinet* (Palo Alto, CA: Stanford University Press, 1997), 185.
23. Clarke, *Tao of the West,* 109.
24. Wu, *Butterfly as Companion,* 174.
25. Møllgaard, "Zhuangzi's Religious Ethics," 367.

Conclusion: Be Ordinary

1. Kuang-ming Wu, *The Butterfly as Companion: Meditations on the First Three Chapters of the Chuang Tzu* (New York: State University of New York Press, 1990), 376.
2. Chuang Tzu, *Wandering on the Way: Early Taoist Tales and Parables of Chuang Tzu,* trans. Victor Mair (Honolulu: University of Hawai'i Press, 1994), 52.
3. Jasmin Lee Cori, *Freefall to the Beloved: Mystical Poetry for God's Lovers* (Boulder, CO: Golden Reed, 1996), 111. Reprinted with permission.

Appendix A: Chuang Tzu: Historical Background

1. Wing-tsit Chan, comp. and trans., *A Source Book in Chinese Philosophy* (Princeton, NJ: Princeton University Press, 1963), 17.
2. Ibid., 17–19.
3. Ibid., 213–31.

4. Ibid., 214. After the Chou era, Mo Ti and his teachings were forgotten until recent time due to the lack of intellectual tone.
5. Ibid., 251–52.
6. Mencius opposed the egoistic self-preservation of Yang Chu strongly. He idolized Confucius and was the pupil of Confucius' grandson Tzu-ssu's pupil. Like Confucius, Mencius believed that human nature is good but went a step further in stating that human nature is originally good and had the potential to fulfill the innate goodness. Ibid., 49–50.
7. Although the name Yang Chu had not been mentioned by Mo Ti, by the time of Mencius, he had become as influential as the Mohists. In the words of Mencius: "The words of Yang Chu and Mo Ti fill the world." Cited by Fung Yu-lan, *A Short History of Chinese Philosophy: A Systematic Account of Chinese Thought from Its Origin to the Present Day*, ed. Derk Bodde (New York: Free Press, 1948), 61.
8. Wing-tsit Chan, comp. and trans., *A Source Book in Chinese Philosophy* (Princeton: Princeton University Press, 1963), 309.
9. The name Lieh Tzu is connected with Negative Taoism and is often spoken of in connection with Yang Chu and his egoism of "not plucking the hair." Negative Taoism takes refuge in the negative aspect of Taoist philosophy to the point of embracing passivity and noninvolvement without striving for balance. Chan, *Source Book in Chinese Philosophy*, 309–13.
10. Yu-lan, *Short History of Chinese Philosophy*, 63.
11. Chuang tzu, *Chuang tzu: The Seven Inner Chapters and Other Writings from the Book Chuang tzu*, trans. A. C. Graham (London: George Allen & Unwin), 5. Although Lao Tzu is known as the founder of Taoism, the name Taoist was not attested to him until late in the third century BCE.

Appendix B: The Psychology of Nondoing

1. Allen Watts, *Tao: The Watercourse Way* (New York: Pantheon Books, 1975), 90.
2. This concept can be applied directly toward the understanding of the writings of Chuang Tzu. According to Chuang Tzu, cognitivism "fosters irrelevance to life, and manifests itself in irresponsible mystical abandonment of the self and of the world." Cognitivism uproots a person from his surroundings and contexts. Kuang-ming Wu,

Chuang Tzu: World Philosopher at Play (New York: Crossroad Publishing, 1965), 4–5.
3. Stanley Cavell, *In Quest of the Ordinary: Lines of Skepticism and Romanticism* (Chicago: University of Chicago Press, 1988), 48.
4. Wu, *Chuang Tzu: World Philosopher at Play*, 30–31.
5. Reinhold Niebuhr, *The Essential Reinhold Niebuhr: Selected Essays and Addresses*, ed. Robert McAfee Brown (New Haven, CT: Yale University Press, 1987), 251.
6. Cited by Melody Beattie in *Codependent No More: How to Stop Controlling Others and Start Caring for Yourself* (New York: Harper and Row, 1987), 126–27. See also "Delayed, inhibited, or denied grief," in Harold Kaplan, Benjamin Sadock, and Jack Grebb, *Kaplan and Sadock's Synopsis of Psychiatry: Behavioral Sciences Clinical Psychiatry*, 7th ed. (Baltimore: Williams & Wilkins, 1994), 82–83.
7. Lao Tzu, *Tao Te Ching: A New English Version*, trans. Stephen Mitchell (New York: Harper and Row, 1988), 50. Greg Johanson and Ron Kurtz, *Grace Unfolding: Psychotherapy in the Spirit of the Tao-te Ching* (New York: Bell Tower, 1991), 97.
8. Chuang Tzu, *The Texts of Taoism: The Tao Te Ching, The Writings of Chuang-Tzu and the Thai-Shang*, trans. James Legge (New York: Julian Press, 1959), 339.
9. I employ the term "concept" for the lack of a better word, but in actuality Taoists believe that the essence of this philosophy cannot be conceptualized, or as Chaunt-tzu puts it, "It may be attained but not seen" (Felt but not conceived, intuited but not categorized, divined but not explained). Watts, *Tao*, 42.
10. Ibid., 41.
11. Cited in ibid., *Tao*, 38.
12. Chuang Tzu, *The Texts of Taoism*, 5.
13. Kaplan, Sadock, and Grebb, *Synopsis of Psychiatry*, 83.
14. Paul Meir, *Don't Let Jerks Get the Best of You: Advice for Dealing with Difficult People* (Petaling Jaya, Malaysia: Castle Book, 1993), 103.
15. Charles Morris, *Psychology: An Introduction* (Upper Saddle River, NJ: Prentice Hall, 1973), 439–40.
16. Hans-Georg Gadamer, *Philosophical Hermeneutics*, trans. and ed. David E. Linge (Berkeley: University of California Press, 1976), 49.
17. T. L. Orcutt and J. R. Prell, *Integrative Paradigms in Psychotherapy* (Columbus, OH: Allyn and Bacon, 1994), 63.
18. Wu, *Chuang Tzu: World Philosopher at Play*, 17.
19. Johanson and Kurtz, *Grace Unfolding*, 9–10.
20. Watts, *Tao*, 21.

21. Ibid., chapter 22.
22. Paul Tillich, *Systematic Theology*, vol. 1 (New York: SCM, 1951), 198.
23. Ibid., 199. Tillich further suggests that the tension between finite individualization and finite participation is the basis of many psychological and sociological problems, and it is therefore an important topic for depth psychology to look into. At the ontological level, there is a tension between loneliness and belonging. Besides the expression of the concept of ontological polarity in individualization and participation, Tillich also speaks of the polar conflict within reason. The polarity of structure and depth in reason leads to conflict between autonomous and heteronous reason. The polarity of the static and dynamic produces a conflict between absolutism, and relativism and the polarity of the formal and the emotional elements results in the conflict between formalism and irrationalism. These conflicts lead ultimately to the quest for union and mystery. Ibid., 83.
24. Cited by Fritjof Capra in *Tao of Physics: An Exploration of the Parallels between Modern Physics and Eastern Mysticism* (New York: Bantam, 1984), 132. The significance of this concept in relation to human psyche is that it allows one to see unity in opposition and thus resolves "conflict" within oneself. Prolonged conflict leads to neurochemical changes. In their study of gamma-aminobytyric acid (GABA), Peterson, Maier, and Seligman point out that GABA receptors produce inhibition by allowing chloride to enter the neuron. The negative charge produces chloride ions, which results in the hyperpolarization of the neuron. Hyperpolarization in turn reduces the excitation within the cell. Benzodiazepines are one of the most notable binding sites. They exert their effect by facilitating the transmission of GABA. Benzodiazepines help increase the number of chloride channel openings, which results in the reduction of anxiety and fear and seizure activity in the brain. In the study of the role of GABA, Peterson, Maier, and Seligman discover that animals that had been exposed to inescapable shock showed reduced levels of GABA. This discovery implies that uncontrollable events lead to the disruption of the task of problem-solving, affecting one's emotion, aggression, and physiology. Further, the level of "control" is, according to the researchers, determined by one's explanatory style. Christopher Peterson, Steven F. Maier, and Martin E. P. Seligman, *Learned Helplessness: A Theory for the Age of Personal Control* (New York: Oxford University Press, 1993), 67–68.
25. *Tao Te Ching*, chapter 37.
26. Cited by Watts, *Tao*, 38. See also Suzuki's "Introduction," in Chuang Tzu, *The Text of Taoism*, 24–25.

27. Watts, *Tao,* 76.
28. Ibid, 88.
29. Wu, *Chuang Tzu: World Philosopher at Play,* 17.
30. Edwin H. Friedman, "Bowen Theory and Therapy." In *Handbook of Family Therapy,* ed. Alan S. Gurman and David P. Kniskern, vol. 2 (New York: Brunner/Mazel, 1991), 161.
31. Ibid.
32. Wu, *Chuang Tzu: World Philosopher at Play,* 82.
33. Friedman, "Bowen Theory and Therapy," 152.
34. *Tao Te Ching,* chapter 40.
35. Johanson and Kurtz, *Grace Unfolding,* 5.

Bibliography

Allinson, Robert E. *Chuang-Tzu for Spiritual Transformation.* New York: State of New York University Press, 1989.

Ames, Roger. "Introduction." In *Yuan Dao: Tracing Dao to Its Source,* translated by D. C. Lau and Roger T. Ames. New York: Ballantine Book, 1998.

Beattie, Melody. *Codependent No More: How to Stop Controlling Others and Start Caring for Yourself.* New York: Harper & Row, 1987

Bernstein, Richard. *Beyond Objectivism and Relativism: Science, Hermeneutics and Praxis.* Philadelphia: University of Pennsylvania, 1983.

Bonhoeffer, Dietrich. *Ethics.* New York: MacMillan, 1955.

Buscaglia, Leo. *Living, Loving, and Learning.* New York: Fawcett Columbine, 1982.

Capra, Fritjof. *The Tao of Physics: An Exploration of the Parallels between Modern Physics and Eastern Mysticism.* New York: Bantam, 1984.

Carr, Janet K., and Marian C. Eberly. "Nutrition Philosophy." *The Remuda Review: The Christian Journal of Eating Disorders* 2, no. 2 (2003): 1–2.

Cavell, Stanley. *In Quest of the Ordinary: Lines of Skepticism and Romanticism.* Chicago: University of Chicago Press, 1988.

Chan, Wing-tsit, comp. and trans. *A Source Book in Chinese Philosophy.* Princeton, NJ: Princeton University Press, 1963.

Chuang Tzu. *Chuang Tzu: Basic Writings.* Translated by Burton Watson. New York: Columbia University Press, 1996.

———. *Chuang-tzu: The Seven Inner Chapters and Other Writings from the Book Chuang-tzu,* Translated by Angus Charles Graham. London: George Allen & Unwin, 1981.

———. *The Texts of Taoism: The Tao Te Ching, The Writings of Chuang Tzu and the Thai-Shang.* Translated by James Legge. New York: Julian Press, 1959.

———. *The Way of Chuang Tzu.* Translated by Thomas Merton. New York: New Direction, 1965.

Clarke, J. J. *The Tao of the West: Western Transformations of Taoist Thought.* New York: Routlege, 2000.

Claro, Joe, ed. *The Random House Book of Jokes and Anecdotes.* New York: Random House, 1990.

Copleston, Frederick Charles. *A History of Philosophy: The British Philosophers.* Vol. 5, part 2. New York: Image Books, 1959.

Cori, Jasmin. *Freefall to the Beloved: Mystical Poetry for God's Lover.* Boulder, CO: Golden Reed, 1996.

Creel, H. G. *What Is Taoism? And Other Studies in Chinese Cultural History.* Chicago: University of Chicago Press, 1970.

Disney Enterprises. *Disney's Toy Story.* Burbank, CA: Disney Enterprises, 1996.

Dourley, J. P. *The Psyche as Sacrament: A Comparative Study of C. G. Jung and Paul Tillich.* Toronto: Inner City Books, 1981.

Friedman, Edwin H. "Bowen Theory and Therapy." In *Handbook of Family Therapy.* Vol. 2, edited by Alan S. Gurman and David Kniskern. New York: Brunner/Mazel, 1991.

Gadamer, Hans-Georg. *Philosophical Hermeneutics.* Translated and edited by David E. Linge. Berkeley: University of California Press, 1976.

Hedaya, Robert J. *Understanding Biological Psychiatry.* New York: Norton, 1996.

Hilllman, James. *The Soul's Code: In Search of Character and Calling.* New York: Warner Books, 1997.

Johanson, Greg, and Ron Kurtz. *Grace Unfolding: Psychotherapy in the Spirit of the Tao-te Ching.* New York: Bell Tower, 1991.

Kaplan, Harold, Benjamin Sadock, and Jack Grebb. *Kaplan and Sadock's Synopsis of Psychiatry: Behavioral Sciences Clinical Psychiatry.* 7th ed. Baltimore: Williams and Wilkins, 1994.

Kelcher, Jewel. *A Knight Without Armor.* New York: HarperEntertainment, 1999.

Kramer, Peter. *Listening to Prozac.* New York: Viking, 1993.

Krishnamurti, J. *In the Light of Silence, All Problems Are Dissolved: Excerpts from J. Krishnamurti's Talks and Writings.* Chennai: Krishnamurti Foundation India, 1992.

Lao Tzu. *Tao Te Ching.* Translated by D. C. Lau. Baltimore: Penguin Books, 1963.

———. *Tao Te Ching: A New English Version*. Translated by Stephen Mitchell. New York: Harper and Row, 1988.

———. *Way of Life: A New Translation of the Tao Te Ching*. Translated by Raymond B. Blackney. New York: New American Library, 1955.

Mair, Victor. *Wandering on the Way: Early Taoist Tales and Parables of Chuang Tzu*. Honolulu: University of Hawai'i Press, 1994.

Mashi, Y. A. *Critical History of Modern Philosophy*. Delhi: Montilal Banarsidass, 1975.

May, Gerald. *Simply Sane*. New York: Crossroad, 1977.

Meir, Paul. *Don't Let Jerks Get the Best of You: Advice for Dealing with Difficult People*. Petaling Jaya (Malaysia): Castle Book, 1993.

Merton, Thomas. *Mystics and Zen Masters*. New York: Noonday Press, 1967.

———, trans. *The Way of Chuang Tzu*. New York: New Direction, 1965.

Moore, G. E. *Philosophical Studies*. London: Routledge & Kegan Paul, 1951.

Moore, Thomas. *Soul Mates: Honoring the Mysteries of Love and Relationship*. New York: HarperPerennial, 1994.

Møllgaard, Eske. "Zhuangzi's Religious Ethics." *American Academy of Religion* 71, no. 2 (2003): 366.

Morris, Charles. *Psychology: An Introduction*. Upper Saddle River, NJ: Prentice Hall, 1973.

Orcutt, T. L., and J. R. Prell. *Integrative Paradigms of Psychotherapy*. Columbus, OH: Allyn and Bacon, 1994.

Panikkar, Raimundo. *A Dwelling Place of Wisdom*. Translated by Annemarie S. Kidder. Louisville, KY: Westminster/John Knox Press, 1993.

Peterson, Christopher, Steven F. Maier, and Martin E. P. Seligman. *Learned Helplessness: A Theory for the Age of Personal Control*. New York: Oxford University Press, 1993.

Reid, Daniel. *The Tao of Health, Sex, and Longevity: A Modern Practical Guide to the Ancient Way*. New York: Simon & Schuster, 1989.

Robinet, Isabella. *Taoism: Growth of a Religion, a Translation and Adaptation by Phyllis Brooks of Robinet* (Palo Alto, CA: Stanford University Press, 1997), 185.

Song, C. S. *Theology from the Womb of Asia*. New York: Orbis Books, 1986.

Sorajjakool, Siroj. *Child Prostitution in Thailand: Listening to Rahab*. New York: Haworth Press, 2003.

———. *Wu Wei, Negativity, and Depression: The Principle of Non-trying in the Practice of Pastoral Care*. New York: Haworth Pastoral Press, 2001.

Tillich, Paul. *Systematic Theology.* Vol. 1. New York: SCM, 1951.

Ulanov, Ann Belford. *Finding Space: Winnicott, God, and Psychic Reality.* Louisville, KY: Westminster John Knox, 2001.

Watson, Burton, trans. *Chuang Tzu: Basic Writings.* New York: Columbia University Press, 1996.

Watts, Alan. *Tao: The Watercourse Way.* New York: Pantheon Books, 1975.

Winnicott, D. W. *Playing and Reality.* London: Tavistock, 1971.

Wright, Arthur F., ed. *Studies in Chinese Thought.* Chicago: University of Chicago Press, 1953.

Wu, Kuang-ming. *The Butterfly as Companion: Meditations on the First Three Chapters of the Chuang Tzu.* New York: State University of New York Press, 1990.

———. *Chuang Tzu: World Philosopher at Play.* New York: Crossroad Publishing, 1965.

Young, Richard. *Paths of a Prodigal: Explorations into the Deeper Reaches of Spiritual Living.* New York: Larson Publications, 1997.

Yu-lan, Fung. *A Short History of Chinese Philosophy: A Systematic Account of Chinese Thought from Its Origin to the Present Day.* Edited by Derk Bodde. New York: Free Press, 1948.

Index